Enacting Diverse Learning Environments
Improving the Climate for Racial/Ethnic
Diversity in Higher Education

Sylvia Hurtado, Jeffrey Milem, Alma Clayton-Pedersen, and Walter Allen

ASHE-ERIC Higher Education Report Volume 26, Number 8

Prepared by

ERIC Clearinghouse on Higher Education
The George Washington University
URL: www.eriche.org

In cooperation with

Association for the Study
of Higher Education
URL: http://www.tiger.coe.missouri.edu/~ashe

Published by

Graduate School of Education and Human [
The George Washington University
URL: www.gwu.edu

Adrianna J. Kezar, Series Editor

Cite as

Hurtado, Sylvia, Jeffrey Milem, Alma Clayton-Pedersen, and Walter Allen. 1999. *Enacting Diverse Learning Environments: Improving the Climate for Racial/Ethnic Diversity in Higher Education.* ASHE-ERIC Higher Education Report Volume 26, No. 8. Washington, D.C.: The George Washington University, Graduate School of Education and Human Development.

Library of Congress Catalog Card Number 99-61138
ISSN 0884-0040
ISBN 1-878380-88-5

Managing Editor: Lynne J. Scott
Manuscript Editor: Barbara M. Fishel
Cover Design by Michael David Brown, Inc., The Red Door Gallery, Rockport, ME

The ERIC Clearinghouse on Higher Education invites individuals to submit proposals for writing monographs for the *ASHE-ERIC Higher Education Report* series. Proposals must include:

1. A detailed manuscript proposal of not more than five pages.
2. A chapter-by-chapter outline.
3. A 75-word summary to be used by several review committees for the initial screening and rating of each proposal.
4. A vita and a writing sample.

ERIC Clearinghouse on Higher Education
Graduate School of Education and Human Development
The George Washington University
One Dupont Circle, Suite 630
Washington, DC 20036-1183

> *The mission of the ERIC system is to improve American education by increasing and facilitating the use of educational research and information on practice in the activities of learning, teaching, educational decision making, and research, wherever and whenever these activities take place.*

This publication was prepared partially with funding from the Office of Educational Research and Improvement, U.S. Department of Education, under contract no. ED-99-00-0036. The opinions expressed in this report do not necessarily reflect the positions or policies of OERI or the Department.

EXECUTIVE SUMMARY

Research over the years has begun to provide important guidance in understanding how to achieve diversity while improving the social and learning environments for students from different racial/ethnic backgrounds. One key to enacting diverse learning environments lies in understanding and developing programs and policies to improve the campus climate for racial/ethnic diversity, which involves understanding the environment from the perspectives of members from different racial/ethnic backgrounds, creating opportunities for improved race relations that permeate the classroom and extracurricular lives of students, and realizing the educational benefits of diverse learning environments for students who will need to be prepared to meet the demands of a complex, diverse society. Given the extensive effort and progress colleges and universities have made toward diversification in the last 20 to 30 years, it is important to reflect on how learning and educational objectives can be maximized.

What Is the Campus Climate for Racial/Ethnic Diversity?

To improve the climate, one must conceptualize it in relation to racial/ethnic diversity so that its impact can be assessed. In higher education research, the campus climate has been defined as the current perceptions, attitudes, and expectations that define the institution and its members (Peterson and Spencer 1990). These common attitudes and perceptions have been conceptualized as malleable and distinguishable from the stable norms and beliefs that may constitute an organizational culture. This perspective of the climate is modified by researchers who have begun to systematically assess the climate by examining the perceptions and attitudes of various groups on campus, and it is greatly enhanced by theories of race relations and social psychology when the psychological climate is related to racial/ethnic diversity. These theories present the notion that quite diverse views of the environment emerge as a result of racial dynamics that develop on a campus. Theories of race relations and racial attitudes assist us in understanding why an individual or group may hold a particular view of the environment. Moreover, although traditional notions of climate have focused on the psychological dimension, it is linked with a historical legacy of exclusion at the institution, its structural diversity, and behaviors on campus that include interactions inside and outside the classroom.

These aspects of the institutional context are informed by changes in government and policy and the larger forces of sociohistorical change in our society. This framework provides a sense of how racial/ethnic diversity permeates many aspects of a campus environment and the many ways in which researchers have attempted to capture aspects of the issue of diversity on campus. A key finding emerging from this literature is that each aspect of this framework is connected with each other. That is, campuses can no longer speak about changes in the number of diverse students without recognizing how this change affects the psychological climate or opportunities for interaction across different groups on campus—and ultimately changes in educational outcomes for students.

What Impact Does the Climate for Diversity Have on Students?

An important principle underlying this conceptualization of the climate for diversity is that different racial/ethnic groups often view the campus differently, a fact that has been confirmed in numerous studies. Further, each conception is valid because it has real consequences for the individual (Astin 1968; Tierney 1987). In this regard, it is realistic to find research studies in which some elements of the climate may have more salience for particular groups and therefore take on more importance in students' lives as a result. Therefore, *Enacting Diverse Learning Environments* attempts to draw from studies on many different racial/ethnic groups to provide a balanced portrait of how different groups view the campus climate and experience its effects. It also brings to light some of the lesser known studies to connect them with the more widely read theory and research in higher education, psychology, and sociology. Moreover, both researchers and educators must acknowledge there is much to be learned from research conducted on specific groups, including African-American, Asian Pacific–American, Latino, Native American, and white students. Overall, the literature reveals how the different, interrelated aspects of the climate for diversity are linked with a broad range of educational outcomes for diverse groups of students.

First, the research shows that increasing the racial/ethnic diversity on a campus while neglecting to attend to the racial climate can result in difficulties for students of color as well as for white students. Research has documented well how different racial/ethnic groups can experience difficulties as a result of a poor racial climate. This research shows that individuals' and particular groups' perceptions of the environment are not inconsequential or intangible, but have tangible and real effects on the transition to college and on educational outcomes. Second, many studies indicate the importance of having diverse peers in the learning environment for important outcomes, such as improvements in students' ability to engage in more complex thinking about problems and to consider multiple perspectives, and improvements in intergroup relations and understanding. Harnessing the learning that can be achieved through contact in student peer groups is key. Third, additional empirical studies reveal that, under certain optimal conditions, racial conflict can be minimized and learning environments enhanced by diversity. Much of this work suggests that providing opportunities for quality interaction and an overall climate of support results not only in a better racial climate but also in important learning outcomes for students. In many ways, racial/ethnic diversity is linked with institutional goals for learning and teaching.

How Can the Climate for Racial/Ethnic Diversity Be Improved to Enhance the Learning Environment?

Improving the climate may require some fundamental institutional changes. Most basic is a conceptual shift in thinking about how diversity is central to the institution's overall priorities for teaching and learning, which also requires a change in how students are regarded or valued. Twelve principles derived from the research can become central in campus initiatives to improve the climate for racial/ethnic diversity. It begins with an articulation of how diversity is central to education and continues with self-examination. Second, institutions can structure opportunities for increased interaction and involvement among students from diverse racial/ethnic groups in the classroom and outside the classroom. A limited number of examples of promising practices in *Enacting Diverse Learning Environments* attempt to realize the potential benefits of racially/ethnically diverse student environments and intentionally create opportunities for learning and interacting across communities of difference.

CONTENTS

FOREWORD

Diversity, multiculturalism, access, race/ethnicity, and campus climate have become common words and part of our national dialogue on higher education. Orientation programs, first-year courses, introductory disciplinary courses, and residence hall programs have all begun to emphasize how important diversity is. National task forces, such as the National Task Force for Minority Achievement in Higher Education sponsored by the Education Commission of the States, are shaping states' policies designed to improve racial or ethnic environments. Accrediting agencies have begun to link diversity with standards for accreditation. And many national higher education associations have begun conducting research and developing programs to foster more positive environments for various underrepresented groups in higher education. A notable example is the Association of American Colleges and Universities's annual conference and its website that addresses diversity: *http://www.inform.umd.edu/diversityweb*. In addition, the Office of Minorities in Higher Education at the American Council on Education produces an annual status report on minorities that addresses institutions' structural diversity. These collective activities illustrate the momentum building to improve racial and ethnic environments on our college campuses.

Proponents herald the various outcomes of diversity—from retention to academic achievement to improved learning outcomes for students—yet limited evidence is available to explain why diversity in general, and racial or ethnic diversity in particular, enhances students' experiences and meets institutional goals. Although many individuals can anecdotally attest to the impact, this response often does not satisfy skeptical policy makers, administrators, faculty, or students. Recently, those who are skeptical have initiated policies to restrict the impact of race or ethnicity in decision making (Proposition 209 and efforts to eliminate affirmative action). *Enacting Diverse Learning Environments* provides the evidence about the benefits of diversity and specifically looks at the impact of positive racial or ethnic environments on students' learning—the core mission of college campuses. The authors draw on years of research on existing programs and practices. Their primary objective is "to provide college administrators, faculty, and students with information from recent and classic research studies that can guide them in improving the climate for diversity on their campuses." National, statewide, and institutional programs and initiatives will benefit from this comprehensive synthesis.

Sylvia Hurtado, associate professor at the Center for the Study of Higher and Postsecondary Education, University of Michigan, Jeffrey Milem, assistant professor in the College of Education, University of Maryland–College Park, Alma Clayton-Pedersen, assistant to the provost and assistant professor, Vanderbilt University, and Walter Allen, professor of sociology, University of California at Los Angeles, all have significant experience in research on issues of racial and ethnic environments. Their collective expertise from various disciplines makes this volume an authoritative source. The authors develop a conceptualization of the campus climate, a much-needed foundation for planned change in practice or policy. They describe how "central to the conceptualization of a campus climate for diversity is the notion that students are educated in distinct racial contexts where learning and socializing occur," and proceed to review the history of exclusion in higher education. Climate can be examined through various components, and the authors examine the impact of *structural diversity* (the number of underrepresented students on a campus), the *psychological climate* (prejudice), and *behavioral dimensions* (relations among students, an instructor's pedagogical approach). Next, they review state, federal (through financial aid), and institutional efforts to improve racial or ethnic diversity. They delineate 12 principles that can be used to transform campuses into more positive racial/ethnic environments. One of the principles, collaborative and cooperative learning, can be explored in greater detail in an ASHE-ERIC monograph, *Cooperative Learning,* by David Johnson, Roger Johnson, and Karl Smith. Another principle, creating supportive out-of-classroom experiences, is reviewed in another ASHE-ERIC monograph, *Student Learning Outside the Classroom: Transcending Artificial Boundaries,* by George Kuh, Katie Branch Douglas, Jon Lund, and Jackie Ramin-Gyurnek. The last section of the monograph on promising practices provides a wealth of detailed examples for campuses to draw upon. I was fortunate enough to be at the University of Michigan when the Office of Intergroup Relations, Conflict, and Community hosted the Intergroup Dialogues. These dialogues had a profound impact on my own understanding of racial and ethnic environments.

Improving the climate for ethnic and racial minorities on campuses has often been characterized as a goal, but it has not yet been seen as an imperative. The research highlighted in *Enacting Diverse Learning Environments* will make readers aware that the mission of the institution itself—learning—is tied to improving the racial/ethnic climate. The close link between campus climate and the teaching and learning processes should have a profound impact on the priority placed on addressing issues of campus climate.

Realizing the promise of an improved racial/ethnic environment will most likely mean fundamental change to the institution. The type of comprehensive, intentional change necessary may require modification of core processes. Barbara Curry's ASHE-ERIC monograph, *Instituting Enduring Innovations,* could be a helpful resource.

It is truly remarkable what a group of dedicated individuals can create. I also want to thank the Common Destiny Alliance (CODA) and the committed authors of this book for spending years synthesizing the literature. Their persistence in conducting and synthesizing studies to provide needed answers for policy and practice should not be understated.

Adrianna J. Kezar
Series Editor,
Assistant Professor of Higher Education, and
Director, ERIC Clearinghouse on Higher Education

ACKNOWLEDGMENTS

This report began as a project of several scholars brought together by the Common Destiny Alliance (CODA), a consortium of organizations and scholars who care about and work to end prejudice and practices that separate rather than unite the people of this country. The alliance seeks to encourage and assist child advocates, policy makers, school systems, colleges and universities, businesses, and others to view racial and ethnic diversity as a resource that can help our nation attain such goals as improving economic productivity and the academic achievement of all learners. CODA identifies and promotes social policies and practices, especially those related to education, that encourage racial and ethnic understanding and cooperation as well as capitalize on the potential for learning that diversity provides. It is an ongoing national effort to organize and sustain collective action that will result in organizations', scholars', and individual practitioners' working to end policies and practices that separate us rather than unite us. The Lilly Endowment, the George Gund Foundation, the Ford Foundation, and the Carnegie Corporation of New York have funded the alliance's activities.

With the support of CODA, the authors met in Los Angeles with a consensus panel of scholars and practitioners who have conducted research on race relations or have been centrally involved with racial/ethnic concerns in higher education. The members of the panel offered a critical review of the initial draft of the report. Over the course of the three-day meeting, panel members made valuable suggestions about ways to strengthen the report. The consensus panel included Hector Garza, vice president, Division of Access and Equity Programs, Office of Minorities in Higher Education at the American Council on Education; Marsha Hirano-Nakanishi, director of the Office of Analytic Studies in the Office of the Chancellor of the California State University System; and Gail Thomas, professor of sociology who was then director of the Race and Ethnic Studies Institute at Texas A&M University.

Both CODA and the University of Michigan helped to fund the contributions of graduate students who were involved with aspects of the report. We wish to thank graduate assistant Sybril M. Brown Bennett, Vanderbilt University, and Karen Kurotsuchi Inkelas, Christine Navia, and numerous other graduate students at the University of Michigan who read versions of the report and commented on it. The

---

authors also wish to recognize the generous financial support provided for the work of CODA through the Lilly Endowment and the personal support of former education program directors Joan Lipsitz and Samuel D. Cargile. Finally, we wish to thank the anonymous reviewers, and Adrianna Kezar and members of the staff at ASHE-ERIC, who remained enthusiastic about this manuscript and cheerfully awaited its final draft.

INTRODUCTION

Higher education institutions must improve the climate for diversity on campus if they are to increase the number of baccalaureate degrees awarded in support of the national economy. By 2010, students of color will make up 24 percent of the population 18 and under, with close to half of this age category consisting of students of color in several key states (D.J. Carter and Wilson 1993). Although record college enrollments were reported for racial/ethnic minorities at the beginning of the 1990s, the gaps in the college participation rate and attainment levels among white, African-American, and Latino students have actually widened over the last decade (D.J. Carter and Wilson 1996). Moreover, enrollments for American Indians, Latinos, and African Americans have grown primarily at two-year colleges, where entering students are less likely to eventually attain a baccalaureate degree (Bernstein and Eaton 1994). Thus, growth in college enrollments has not necessarily translated into equitable representation in higher education across the tiers of postsecondary institutions. While the contexts of home and school socialization continue to shape opportunities for college attendance, the challenge of recruiting, retaining, and providing a satisfying college experience for an increasingly diverse student population rests with higher education.

This report was written on the assumption that achieving diversity and educational equity will remain one of higher education's primary goals as we move into the next millennium. It focuses specifically on important principles derived from research on diversity at postsecondary institutions. The research reviewed suggests that an institution's ability to provide a comfortable environment for learning and socializing is a key factor in facilitating the intellectual and social development of all students. The monograph addresses the multiple sources and outcomes of a campus climate for diversity to provide a better understanding of students' experiences at institutions that are learning how to become multicultural environments.

The primary objective of this report is to provide college administrators, faculty, and students with information from recent and classic research studies that can guide them in improving the climate for diversity on their campuses. Because understanding how we construct our environments is an important step toward improving them for students' success, the first part of this report synthesizes findings from research and the literature on the campus climate for diversity, the experiences of various racial/ethnic groups, and how the climate affects educational outcomes. It addresses, in the next six sections, a framework for research, the historical legacy of inclusion or exclusion, the impact of structural diversity, the psychological climate, the behavioral dimension, and the roles of state policy and financial aid in ensuring diversity. The second part of the monograph presents specific design principles derived from empirical research to assist institutions in improving the climate for diversity, focusing on those principles that the research has shown work with diverse populations. Although some of the principles may require some fundamental institutional changes, most of these principles can be translated into specific programs and practices on a variety of college campuses. The monograph concludes with information on a select group of programs, some typical and others very distinctive, that exemplify the identified principles and proactively address the emerging issues of the climate confronting diverse college student populations.

CONCEPTUALIZING THE CAMPUS CLIMATE FOR DIVERSITY

A great deal of research on various racial/ethnic students in higher education focuses on an array of cognitive and affective outcomes and group differences in educational attainments (see Durán 1983, Pascarella and Terenzini 1991, and Sedlacek 1987 for comprehensive reviews). Although these earlier research syntheses reflect a critical part of the scholarly work on various racial/ethnic students in higher education, they include almost no specific references to the potential influence of the institutional climate for diversity. The reason for the lack of references may be that some view the climate for racial/ethnic diversity as important for students, yet believe it is too difficult to comprehend or too intangible to assess (Crosson 1988; M. Green 1989). Recent research has begun to change this view as both qualitative and quantitative researchers engage in work that asks students, faculty, and administrators directly about their perceptions of the institution's climate for racial/ethnic diversity, their experiences with diversity initiatives on campus, and their own attitudes about and interactions with others from different racial/ethnic groups. Researchers also have used a variety of measures that now show the climate for diversity varies substantially from one institutional context to another (El-Khawas 1989; Gilliard 1996; Hurtado 1992; Peterson, Blackburn, Gamson, Arce, Davenport, and Mingle 1978). To focus the current synthesis of research, an organizing framework is used to present a multidimensional conceptualization of the campus climate for diversity (Hurtado 1993). This approach is important because, to improve the climate for diversity, campuses must first be able to understand the widespread dimensions of the problem that a relatively poor climate may present.

A framework for understanding the various dimensions of the campus climate provides a conceptual handle for understanding an element of the environment that was once thought too complex to comprehend. The framework presented in Figure 1 makes the observations of institutions and individuals concrete. It represents areas where research has been conducted and, more important, where practical or programmatic solutions can be targeted. Most campuses tend to focus on only one element of the climate—the goal of increasing the numbers of racial/ethnic students on campus. Although it is an important area for institutional effort, the framework reinforces the notion that other elements of the climate also require attention and constitute key areas for focusing efforts to increase diversity. The studies reviewed for this monograph contain specific references to these various dimensions of the climate, focus on its impact on students from different racial/ethnic groups, and capture the experiences or individual perspectives of racial/ethnic groups that have historically been underrepresented in higher education.

FIGURE 1

Elements Influencing the Climate for Racial/Ethnic Diversity

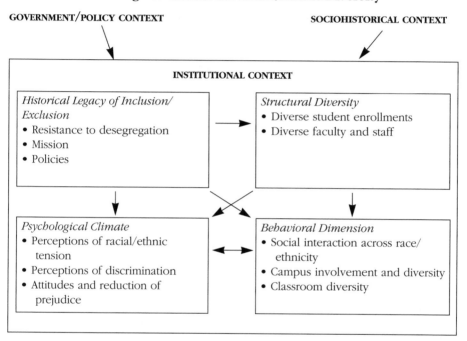

Central to the conceptualization of a campus climate for diversity is the notion that students are educated in distinct racial contexts where learning and socializing occur. These subenvironmental contexts in higher education are shaped by larger external and internal (institutional) contexts. External environmental contexts include the influence of governmental policy, programs, and initiatives as well as the impact of sociohistorical forces.

Examples of governmental and policy contextual factors that may influence the climate for diversity include changing financial aid policies and programs, state and federal policy related to access such as affirmative action, and court decisions related to desegregation of higher education. The review includes a limited amount of literature on aspects of the state's role in promoting the infrastructure of support for diversity initiatives and the role of financial aid in maintaining a diverse student body. Although the primary focus of this report is on what can be done to improve the institutional climate, a review of documents outlining the aspects of the government/policy role in promoting diversity and an improved climate on campus is also included. The current policy environment regarding diversity suggests that states will continue to play an important role in determining what will happen on the nation's public campuses. (This subject could constitute a separate report, and alternative policies should be examined as they directly affect institutions as diverse learning environments.)

Although very little research literature captures the direct impact of some of the external influences on individuals within institutions, the larger sociohistorical context that constitutes support for diversity initiatives affects how institutions respond to diversity as well as how individuals construct their immediate educational environments. It is clear, for example, that changes associated with the entrance of diverse students into higher education would not have occurred without key social movements that accompanied changes in attitudes, heightened awareness about inequality, and intellectual movements of a particular sociohistorical era. Few researchers and only a handful of studies have made an important link with the larger social context and how it influences differences in how faculty perform their role (Lawrence and Blackburn 1985), the impact of college generally (Weidman 1989), or institutional effects on specific types of outcomes we observe for students over time (Dey 1996, 1997). Much more work is needed on the different sociohistorical contexts and their effect on institutions, which in turn, create changes in the outcomes we observe for students. In short, such information would begin to document how institutions simply reflect society or promote progress by producing graduates for a society we aspire to become in the future.

The institutional context is informed by the dynamics of an institution's *historical legacy* of inclusion or exclusion of various racial/ethnic groups, its *structural diversity* in terms of numerical representation of various racial/ethnic groups, the *psychological climate,* which includes perceptions and

Central to the conceptualization of a campus climate for diversity is the notion that students are educated in distinct racial contexts where learning and socializing occur.

attitudes between and among groups, and a *behavioral dimension* that is characterized by relations among groups on campus. Thus, the institutional climate for diversity is conceptualized as a product of these various elements and their dynamics. During the review of research pertinent to each dimension of the climate for diversity, it is important to note that the dimensions are not discrete but connected with each other. For example, the historical vestiges of segregation have an impact on an institution's ability to improve its racial/ethnic student enrollments, and such underrepresentation of specific groups contributes to stereotypical attitudes among individuals, whether at school or work. Some research studies reviewed make these relationships between the various dimensions of climate evident. In short, although some institutions are now taking a multilayered approach to assessing diversity on their campuses and are developing programs to address the climate on campus, very few have taken into account the dynamics of all these important interrelated elements.

This conceptualization is a departure from research that has defined the climate as reflecting participants' common attitudes, perceptions, or observations about the environment (Peterson and Spencer 1990). These common attitudes and perceptions are identified as malleable and distinguishable from the stable norms and beliefs that may constitute an organizational culture. Although this work has been important in distinguishing the climate from the culture of an organization, it is most important in establishing that the climate is malleable and that the current patterns of beliefs and behaviors are amenable to intentional efforts to change or improve the climate. This definition of climate, however, includes the fact that numerous diversity-focused studies of campus climate have consistently shown how distinct various racial/ethnic groups view the climate for diversity on a campus (Abraham and Jacobs 1990; Astin, Treviño, and Wingard 1991; Dey, Rosevear, Navia, and Murphy 1996; Institute 1991). These distinct views disrupt assumptions about common perceptions of the environment that might characterize the psychological climate, suggesting that such notions are not simply psychological in nature but have much to do with a wide range of experiences specific racial/ethnic groups have in society and within institutions. Thus, the current conceptualization extends the view of the psychological climate (perceptions and attitudes) as inherently linked to a range of social phenomena that have to do with structure, history, and actual interactions across diverse communities within the environment. Theories of race relations and racial attitudes further clarify these links (as illustrated by the review of research that follows).

Finally, it is important to note that these different perspectives on the climate for diversity are not only informed by distinct experiences but also are valid because they have real consequences for the individual (Astin 1968; Tierney 1987). This report explores the relationship between the dynamics and multiple ways of assessing the diversity in an environment and their link with educational outcomes for students. Therefore, for each aspect of the conceptual framework one can ask, "How does it ultimately affect students?" We are fortunate now to have a body of research that tells us how each dimension related to diversity is linked with the educational objectives we wish to accomplish for students.

THE HISTORICAL LEGACY OF
INCLUSION OR EXCLUSION

Although some campuses have had a history of admitting and graduating students of color since their founding days, many predominantly white institutions have a history of limited access and exclusion (Thelin 1985). A college's historical legacy of exclusion of various racial and ethnic groups can continue to determine the prevailing climate and influence current practices (Hurtado 1992). Various institutional case studies have documented the historical context and have found that campuses achieve variable degrees of success in creating a supportive climate for students of color (Peterson et al. 1978; Richardson and Skinner 1991). Researchers have found that success often depends on an institution's initial response to the entrance of diverse students and its early establishment of programs to accommodate them; moreover, the response affects or is affected by the institutional philosophy regarding the college's responsibility for educating students of color, its commitment to affirmative action, its intent to offer minority-specific programs, and its attention to the psychological climate and intergroup relations on campus once substantial numbers of students of color are admitted (Peterson et al. 1978). This section focuses on one issue that is particularly tied to the historical context—that is, issues related to the long history of resistance to desegregation in higher education. The need for legal pressures and extended litigation regarding institutional obligations to equitably serve a more diverse group of students has conveyed the message of institutional resistance and, in some cases, outright hostility toward people of diverse backgrounds.

Desegregation and Institutional Mission
Historically black colleges and universities (HBCUs) and American Indian colleges have a historic commitment to serve populations that once were excluded from higher education and continue to face seemingly intractable problems in attaining progress at predominantly white institutions. In recent years, as a result of dramatic changes in enrollments of Latinos, the Hispanic-serving institutions have also begun to emphasize their commitment to educating Latino students. It is impossible to discuss desegregation in higher education without considering the history, role, purpose, and special mission of these institutions. Today, these special-mission institutions not only represent an alternative choice for students, but also view their mission as attending to the cultural

and academic development of students and their respective communities. More racially and ethnically diverse students are educated in predominantly white institutions than in special-mission institutions, however (D.J. Carter and Wilson 1993); thus, state systems' and individual public and private institutions' patterns of response to desegregation pressures become integral in defining campus racial climates. As part of developing a positive response to these issues, it is critical that institutions adopt a clear definition of desegregation and integrate planning for it with overall strategic planning for the institution (Stewart 1991). Further, the goals of desegregation plans must be precisely articulated, with the objective of increasing the overall representation of the historically excluded group. Several studies illustrate the problems that have resulted from multiple definitions of and approaches to desegregation.

A discussion of the findings from an analysis of the effect of *Ayers v. Mabus,* a desegregation case, notes that "a distinction must be made between desegregation and educational equality. Desegregation does not necessarily produce movement toward educational equality. It is a means to a specific end—more and better education for children, youth, and adults—not an end in and of itself" (Blake 1991, p. 555). This study of changes in enrollment patterns in Mississippi over the 10 years from 1976 to 1986 found that enrollments of blacks dropped by 11.2 percent, while those of whites remained stable. Further, the decline in enrollments of black students was felt almost exclusively at the state's historically black colleges. And although black enrollments at predominantly white colleges increased 24 percent, this amount was not high enough to offset the decline at HBCUs.

These findings can be viewed in one of two ways. One perspective would consider the changes in figures with regard to the representation of black Mississippians over the past 40 years and conclude that the state had been able to make much progress over the time period. Black enrollment climbed from 0 percent at the state's predominantly white institutions before the 1954 *Brown* decision to 7.6 percent in 1973 to 13.6 percent in 1986. On the other hand, when one considers that African Americans make up over one-half of the state's precollege population, these gains seem more modest and suggest that little relative progress has been made to reduce the degree of inequality that exists within the higher education system in Mississippi.

Although the desegregation of white colleges has expanded opportunities for African Americans, the losses of opportunity for African Americans at the state's HBCUs have resulted in a greater relative loss of opportunity for African Americans in Mississippi. The "fastest road to desegregated equality versus desegregated inequality" can be found in "enhancing the academic programs and facilities of the desegregating HBCUs and maintaining their numerical strength, while simultaneously taking steps to increase the numbers of black students attending the state's HWCUs [historically white colleges and universities]" (Blake 1991, p. 557).

Some believe the decision in *Adams v. Richardson* was the most important legal decision to affect the achievement of access to higher education and opportunity for blacks for three primary reasons (Thomas and McPartland 1984). First, the desegregation of public predominantly white institutions served to increase the presence of blacks in higher education. Second, the desegregation of predominantly white institutions also served to expand the choice of major fields available to black students. Third, relative to the concerns raised by Blake (1991), the *Adams* mandate sought to provide a broader definition of equality of opportunity in higher education for blacks by insisting that colleges and universities strive to achieve greater representation of students, faculty, and staff of color while also insisting on higher levels of access and retention of students of color. In recognition of the important and special role of HBCUs, the mandate declared that these efforts at desegregation and equity were not to have a detrimental impact on the HBCUs.

The findings of this study (Thomas and McPartland 1984) come from analyses of data on southern institutions* gathered for 1976 to 1978 by the Office of Civil Rights and are similar to Blake's. Desegregation of higher education facilitated the access of black students to predominantly white institutions, but gains in enrollment at predominantly white institutions appear to have occurred at the expense of enrollments at HBCUs. During these years, enrollments for both black and white students declined, but the decline in the enrollment of black students was relatively greater (Thomas and McPartland 1984). Therefore, despite the gains made toward desegrega-

Despite the gains made toward desegregation at these southern institutions, black students' access to higher education actually decreased during this time.

*The institutions are in the states of Alabama, Arkansas, Delaware, Florida, Georgia, Kentucky, Louisiana, Maryland, Mississippi, North Carolina, Oklahoma, South Carolina, Tennessee, Texas, Virginia, and West Virginia.

tion at these southern institutions, black students' access to higher education actually decreased during this time. And these findings all run counter to the conditions mandated in the *Adams* decision (Thomas and McPartland 1984).

The success of legislation and litigation regarding desegregation in higher education has been mixed at best. Numerous reasons are cited, including a lack of enforcement by the federal government. At times, members of the executive and legislative branches appear to have been openly hostile to these issues (Williams 1988). Moreover, with the abandonment of the *Adams* case in 1990 and the current debate regarding affirmative action, we can expect that the federal government will take a much more passive role. Some observers argue that if equity and access are to be ensured, the battle will have to be fought by the states. Given the prevailing sentiment in some states toward affirmative action and equality of opportunity, it is difficult to predict the extent to which visionaries in state governments will be willing to assume this role. Further, even if some state leaders are willing, the capacity for most states to regulate their colleges and universities (particularly their flagship institutions) has been limited (Williams 1988). Hence, it seems that if commitment to desegregation and equality of opportunity in higher education is to be continued, it is most likely to be successful at the level of individual campuses, with provisions for support from the state.

A report by the Southern Education Foundation's Panel on Educational Opportunity and Postsecondary Desegregation (1995) analyzes the potential impact of the Supreme Court's decision in *United States v. Fordyce* on further desegregation in higher education. Panel members persuasively contend that the decision in this case provides us with a new opportunity to desegregate the higher education system and suggest that the wording of the decision in this case seems to have resolved several important questions. For example, the Court recognized the continuous legacy of segregation signified by the persistence of racial inequity in public higher education. Most significantly, the Court's decision confirmed that the 1954 *Brown* decision also applies to higher education. The Court also did not accept the argument that adopting race-neutral policies was an adequate remedy in those states that had previously mandated racial segregation in higher education, and deemed a more proactive approach necessary. Of particular importance to scholars and educators, the Court indicated that remedies to the desegregation problem should be "consistent with sound educational practices," suggesting that the lower courts should defer, to some extent, to educators in making their decisions. The Court affirmed that "vestiges of desegregation must be eliminated systemwide in higher education" (p. xix).

The panel offers three recommendations that can be applied to the transformation of the higher education system. First, it is imperative that these efforts to transform state systems be student-centered. "Systems must be organized to advance the interests and respond to the needs of students rather than the preferences of the institutions created to meet those needs" (p. xix). Students are too frequently blamed for failures that should be attributed to the education system. Second, systems of higher education must take a more comprehensive approach to desegregation and issues of equity in education, which involves promoting "the principle that each sector of education is linked to the others" (p. xix). Panel members point out that "each sector of public education is the creation of the state, and it is the state that is ultimately responsible for its quality and performance" (p. 22). Third, systems of education must also become accountable and performance-driven: "Education must be performance-based and accountable for results" (p. xix). A crucial step in fulfilling this principle is providing for a means of regularly collecting data to monitor performance.

In offering their observations and recommendations, the panel rejects the idea of closing HBCUs to achieve desegregation, contending that HBCUs and predominantly white institutions are the result of "purposeful, state-imposed segregation." Hence, "no set of institutions has any more right than another to survive. The burden of desegregation should not fall exclusively or disproportionately on HBCUs" (p. xix). The question also arises about the inequity of placing the burden for change on HBCUs (E. Davis 1993). "Institutions that retain a specifically black identity will not easily be able to reach the level of integration [that] reflects the population. They are being challenged to change their very character, while historically white schools are being asked only to broaden access" (p. 523).

Compelling evidence shows that African-American students experience success on a number of educational outcomes at HBCUs compared with those who attend predominantly white institutions (Allen 1987, 1992; Allen, Epps, and Haniff 1991; Nettles 1988). It is therefore critical that HBCUs remain an option for students. Some students probably would not enter the higher education system if not for the fact that they have chosen to attend an HBCU, pointing to the need for a better understanding of and support for the process of choosing a college for all students of color and for African-American students in particular. Further, in learning more about the affirming environment at HBCUs and its effect on students, we may find ways to improve the campus racial climate at predominantly white institutions to make them more responsive to and supportive of the needs of all students. Perhaps HBCUs are so successful because they "focus on the success of their students and presume their capacity for the success of their students," "they have many faculty and administrators who provide role models and varieties of perspectives," and "they tend to provide whatever programmatic support is necessary as part of the educational program" (Smith 1989, pp. 52–53). Students are able to learn in an environment in which their race does not function "as a stigma in their performance" (p. 53).

Research on the Effects of Desegregation On Individuals

Not a great deal of research has been conducted specifically regarding the effect of desegregation on individuals in institutions of higher education (Thomas and Brown 1982). To be able to address the subject, however, the authors reviewed studies of desegregation in other sectors of the education system that linked its effects to postsecondary education.

The major limitations of research on school desegregation, based on an analysis and summary of such research done before the early 1980s (Thomas and Brown 1982), found that studies of school desegregation generally lacked clarity regarding the goals and objectives of desegregation. The *implied* goals of desegregation were to "(1) achieve a certain student and faculty racial mix; (2) improve minority achievement; (3) improve race relations; (4) promote the access and retention of minorities at the college and advanced higher education levels; and (5) increase the quality and diversity of job opportunities for minorities" (p. 165). Yet most studies of desegregation lack an appropriate theoretical framework and have lacked appropriate modes of relating the research to those who can implement change (Thomas and Brown 1982). Early studies emphasized achievement theory and other "deficit perspectives" that are highly Eurocentric. Theories that acknowledge cultural differences and areas of tension between majority and minority groups are more appropriate for the study of the effects of desegregation. These theoretical assumptions have implications for practice, and we must find ways to convey research findings in ways that will help the broader community. Finally, this research is limited in that desegregation and equality of opportunity have been defined primarily as black/white issues. The studies have focused on samples of African Americans and/or whites without regard for the increasingly multicultural context on campuses and the experiences of students from other historically underrepresented groups.

The findings of many studies of desegregation indicate that minority segregation that occurs in educational settings tends to be perpetuated over stages of the life cycle and across institutional settings (Braddock 1985). A discussion of the lasting impact of school desegregation asserts that "school desegregation is leading to desegregation in several areas of adult life" (Braddock, Crain, and McPartland 1984, p. 261), including college, social situations, and jobs. The analysis indicates that desegregation changes the attitudes and behaviors of whites as well, which can be found in attitudes that reveal diminishing racial stereotypes and lessened fears of hostile reactions in interracial settings among white adults who were in desegregated settings as children.

"One of the most important aspects of racial segregation is its tendency to perpetuate itself" (Braddock 1985, p. 11). Compelling evidence from the research shows that this pattern holds true for both majority and minority individuals. Much of the work done by Braddock, both individually and with his colleagues, involves tests of two different causal explanations for their research findings. The first causal explanation, *racial demography*, refers to "the observed associations with desegregation [that] are spuriously created by a common ecological factor having nothing to do with individual socialization" (p. 15). In other words, changing circumstances produce the observed differences as opposed to changes in individuals. One such factor involves the increased likelihood of random interracial contact for blacks who live in white communities as compared with blacks who live in black communities. A racial demographic explanation for the patterns of relationships between measures of desegregation would explain these findings as "spurious consequences of the communities' demographic features" (p. 16). *Social-psychological* explanations, however, indicate that changes in the attitudes or behaviors of individuals are the result of intergroup contact. Hence, it is important to include measures of the demographic characteristics of communities to better establish support for the influence of social psychological processes. The findings of several studies offer support for changes in social-psychological processes brought about by changing patterns of desegregation (see, e.g., Braddock 1985; Braddock, Crain, and McPartland 1984; Braddock and McPartland 1989; R. Scott and McPartland 1982).

The results of changing patterns of desegregation are becoming more evident, with resulting patterns of behaviors and interactions that have implications for college and work environments. For example, some research evidence suggests that segregation in elementary and secondary schools is perpetuated in college. Black students who had attended desegregated elementary and secondary schools were also more likely to attend desegregated colleges (Braddock 1980; Braddock and McPartland 1982). Subsequent research evidence reveals that early patterns of school desegregation and community desegregation tend to promote desegregation among adults in work environments (Braddock and McPartland 1989), especially among northern blacks where the relationship between school and community desegregation is much less confounded. Moreover, blacks who had attended desegregated high schools were more likely to receive better grades in college than were blacks who attended segregated high schools (Braddock and Dawkins 1981). Similar findings in another study show a greater likelihood of persistence in college among those blacks who attended desegregated high schools (K. Green 1982). Increasing segregation in high schools in various communities in this country, however, indicates that college may be the first opportunity for students to encounter and interact with someone from a different race or ethnicity.

The historical vestiges of segregated schools and colleges continue to affect the climate for racial and ethnic diversity in many ways on college campuses—for example, resistance to desegregation in communities and specific campus settings, maintenance of old campus policies at predominantly white institutions that best serve a homogeneous population, and attitudes and behaviors that prevent interaction across race and ethnicity. Because they are embedded in a culture of a historically segregated environment, many campuses sustain long-standing benefits for particular student groups, which often go unrecognized (Duster 1993). Desegregation policies in schools and colleges were designed to change the racial and ethnic composition of an environment, improve educational opportunity, and ultimately change the environments of our educational institutions. It is through the diversification of the learning and work environment, or the structural diversity of campus settings, that such changes were thought to occur. The next section examines its impact.

"Structural diversity" refers primarily to the numerical representation of various racial, ethnic, and gender groups on campus. Most institutions tend to focus on numerical representation of various groups as a method of achieving equity, often in response to goals for affirmative action and plans for desegregation. Research supports the notion that increasing an institution's structural diversity is considered the first important step in the process of improving the climate for diversity for several reasons. First, environments with highly skewed distributions of socially and culturally different people are critical in shaping the dynamics of social interaction (Kanter 1977). Campuses with high proportions of white students provide limited opportunities for interaction across race and ethnicity and limit students' learning experiences with diverse groups (Hurtado, Dey, and Treviño 1994). Second, in environments lacking a diverse workforce or population, underrepresented groups are regarded as symbols rather than individuals, or as "tokens." Tokenism contributes to heightened visibility of the underrepresented group, exaggeration of differences among groups, and the distortion of individuals' images to fit existing stereotypes (Kanter 1977). That is, the sheer fact that racial and ethnic students remain minorities in majority white environments contributes to their social stigma (Steele 1992) and can produce the stress that goes with minority status (Prillerman, Myers, and Smedley 1989; Smedley, Myers, and Harrell 1993). Third, an institution's proactive stance in increasing the representation of various racial/ethnic groups conveys the message that the campus maintains a multicultural environment as a high institutional priority. For example, African-American, Chicano, and white students in one study tended to report that commitment to diversity was a high institutional priority on campuses that had relatively high percentages of African-American and Latino students (Hurtado 1990). Thus, research suggests that campuses that increase their racial and ethnic enrollments can significantly improve the college experiences of historically underrepresented groups. Moreover, attaining a diverse student body and hiring diverse faculty result in significantly more opportunities for all students to learn how to deal with others from different cultural backgrounds after college.

Diverse Student Enrollments and Increased Complexity

A series of interviews with students led to the conclusion that having sufficient racial/ethnic enrollments gives potential recruits the impression that the campus is hospitable: "No matter how outstanding the academic institution, ethnic minority students can feel alienated if their ethnic representation on campus is small" (Loo and Rolison 1986, p. 72). Increasing the number of students of color on campus is not without problems, however. The racial/ethnic restructuring of student enrollments can bring about some conflict and resistance among groups, and it can create a need for substantial institutional change. For example, increasing the absolute numbers of or creating a critical mass of racial/ethnic students was historically linked with racially related campus protests during the 1970s (Astin, Astin, Bayer, and Bisconti 1975; Astin and Panos 1971). Undoubtedly, students of color demanded that institutions become more responsive to the needs of racial/ethnic minority groups, and such protests continued to serve as an impetus for change and institutional self-examination (Farrell and Jones 1988). The impact of diverse student enrollments has resulted in pressure for institutional transformation—a transformation that has affected both the academic and the social life of the institution, including such changes as the development of ethnic studies programs, diverse student organizations, specific academic support programs, and multicultural programs (Muñoz 1989; Peterson et al. 1978; Treviño 1992).

Increases in enrollments of diverse students, however, have also become problematic for the white majority and for racial/ethnic minority groups. Race relations theorists hypothesize that the larger the relative size of the minority group, the more likely minority individuals will be in conflict with members of the majority, presumably because they are in competition for limited resources (Blalock 1967). Studies have confirmed that some element of conflict can arise with increases in the enrollments of various groups. For example, on campuses where Asian-American enrollments have increased substantially, Asian Pacific–American students have reported more personal experiences of discrimination than any other group (Asian Pacific 1990). One study of several institutions found that white students tend to perceive racial tension on predominantly white campuses with a relatively high number of African-American enrollments (Hurtado 1992). Results from this study also show, however, that when students feel valued and when faculty and administrators are devoted to their development, they are less likely to report racial/ethnic ten-

"No matter how outstanding the academic institution, ethnic minority students can feel alienated if their ethnic representation on campus is small."

sion on campus. This finding suggests that campuses can minimize racial tension and competition among groups by creating a more student-centered environment. (This point is explained further in "Linking the Institutional Climate for Diversity with the General Learning Environment" on p. 55.)

Research about the effects of diverse student enrollments on a variety of student outcomes suggests that greater structural diversity may be beneficial for students. Specifically, the greater the structural diversity at an institution, the more likely white students are to socialize with students across racial/ethnic groups and the more frequently they are to discuss racial and ethnic issues (Chang 1996). Attending a multicultural campus results in more diverse friendship groups, which in turn is associated with more frequent interracial interaction outside the friendship group (Antonio 1998a). After four years of college, white students attending public universities with relatively high levels of racial diversity showed greater social concern and humanitarian values (Deppe 1989). Recent longitudinal studies also reveal that African-American students increase their aspirations for a degree at predominantly white institutions that have substantial numbers of other African-American students (D.F. Carter 1997; D.F. Carter and Montelongo 1998).

Another researcher found in his study of students at the University of California at Berkeley that the changing enrollments have produced a more complex and interesting set of relationships among students (Duster 1993). As a student body becomes more diverse and the representation of students of color rises on a campus, opportunities for white students to interact with people from different racial and ethnic groups increase. When students of color are not widely represented on campus, however, it is rather easy for white students to avoid interaction with students from other racial and ethnic groups. Conversely, as the representation of students of color increases on a campus, it becomes easier for these students to find peers from their own racial/ethnic group enrolled at the institution, thereby making it easier for them to interact within their own racial/ethnic group. At institutions with low representation of students of color, students from these groups have little choice but to interact extensively across racial/ethnic groups (Hurtado, Dey, and Treviño 1994). That is, greater structural diversity provides students of color with a wider range of social options at their institution, which may help "to create more 'comfortable' institutional spaces for their students" (Chang 1996, p. 171).

Consistent with other studies the authors reviewed, maximizing cross-racial interaction and encouraging ongoing discussions about race are educational practices that are beneficial to students (Chang 1996). When the effects of increased structural diversity for students of color are considered without involvement in these activities, however, students of color are likely to report less overall satisfaction with their college experience (Chang 1996). Thus, increasing only the structural diversity of an institution without considering the influence of each of the other dimensions of the campus racial climate is likely to produce problems for students at these institutions.

Diversifying Faculty on Campus

One key point to increasing diversity in the student body is related to an equally strong commitment to diversifying the faculty. Five reasons for needing to diversify the faculty and staff emerge from the literature on diversity in higher education (Smith 1989). First, faculty of color are able to provide support that benefits students from their particular groups. Students of color are likely to seek out faculty "who are like them" and whom they believe will understand them and the experiences that they are going through as students, greatly reducing their feelings of loneliness, alienation, and isolation as students of color. Second, a diverse faculty and staff serve as important representatives of the commitment that the institution has to issues of diversity. Third, a more diverse faculty and staff serve to create a more comfortable environment for faculty and staff as well. The stresses, strains, and challenges experienced by students at predominantly white institutions are also experienced by members of the faculty and staff. Fourth, a diverse faculty and staff bring more voices and more diverse perspectives "to what is taught, how it is taught, and why it is important to learn, which are contributions that are vital to the institution" (p. 57). Fifth, "a diverse faculty and staff reflect one measure of institutional success for an educational institution in a pluralistic society" (p. 57).

A trend analysis of the effect of affirmative action programs on the diversification of the American professoriat between 1972 and 1989 reveals "some good news and some bad news" (Milem and Astin 1993). Not much had changed with regard to the representation of faculty of color during the 17 years covered in the study. Although modest gains were made in the representation of Asian-American faculty during that time period, African-American, Mexican American, Native American, and Puerto Rican faculty made only negligible gains. Other reports indicate that even gains among Asian-American faculty may be negligible, as growth has occurred primarily among Asian-born faculty and not among Asian-American faculty born in the United States (Suzuki 1994).

On a more positive note, the study indicates progress in the representation of women in the professoriat between 1972 and 1989 (Milem and Astin 1993). Other good news in these findings indicates that faculty as a group had become more aware of and committed to issues of racial/ethnic diversity on campus and in the larger society. Between 1972 and 1989, faculty had become committed to issues of diversity and were more willing to become actively and personally involved, and to assume an institutional role, in addressing these issues. The finding of negligible gains in the representation of faculty of color suggests that, during this 17-year period, hiring and retention practices did not significantly change so that a diverse faculty could be sustained. "Faculty have learned how to talk the talk, but they have not yet learned how to walk the walk" (p. 27).

Taken together, these studies on creating a diverse faculty and student body suggest that the educational success of increasing the structural diversity of an institution is linked with attitudes and practice. Increasing the sheer numbers of racial/ethnic students may not automatically improve the campus climate, because attention to other dimensions of the climate become necessary when the racial/ethnic structure of the social environment changes. Further, unchanging practices thwart attempts to recruit and retain students, and have resulted in minimal increases in faculty of color. At the same time, handling the growth of applicants to specific types of campuses from minority groups will become problematic so long as they make up a growing part of the college-age population. This observation is already true for Asian-American students, where growth in the applicant pools has outpaced admission rates and increases in enrollments on campuses have reportedly caused new forms of backlash (Hsia 1988; Takagi 1992). Although campuses have reacted with programmatic responses to initial increases in students of color, they have uniformly ignored the psychological climate and interpersonal aspects of race relations on campus (Peterson et al. 1978). These dimensions are related to the larger social issues of attitudes, prejudice, and intergroup relations. Each of these areas has a substantial body of social science research, and intergroup relations on college campuses appear to be receiving renewed attention from the media. These areas clearly indicate important dimensions of the climate that represent the next phase for self-study and programming for institutions that wish to move beyond the numbers to improve social attitudes, intergroup relations, and the general quality of life on campus.

THE PSYCHOLOGICAL CLIMATE

The psychological dimension of the climate for diversity involves individuals' views of group relations, institutional responses to diversity, perceptions of discrimination or racial conflict, and attitudes held toward others from different racial/ethnic backgrounds. Before reviewing this literature, it is important to note that studies are beginning to show that racially and ethnically diverse administrators, students, and faculty tend to view the campus climate differently. Thus, an individual's position and power within the organization as well as one's view as "insider" or "outsider" contribute to different views or standpoints (Collins 1986). One study found, for example, that 68 percent of white students thought their university was generally supportive of minority students, while only 28 percent of the African-American and Chicano students thought so (Loo and Rolison 1986). Another study found that students of color were more likely to distinguish between different forms of prejudice and discrimination, whereas white students were less likely to grasp such nuances (Cabrera and Nora 1994). Variations within ethnic groups also occur, depending on the student's background and sense of ethnic identity. For example, one study found that American Indian students who closely held to American Indian values were likely to report more negative racial encounters in college than other students (Huffman 1991). These perceptual differences of the college experience are significant, for perception is both a product of the environment and a potential determinant of future interactions and outcomes (Astin 1968; Tierney 1987). As past and contemporary research reveals, these differing perceptions and experiences have real consequences for individuals.

The Impact of Discrimination and Perceptions Of the Climate on Students

What price is paid for institutional neglect of the psychological climate on campus? What is the result of institutional inaction regarding instances of discrimination or students' persistent perceptions of a poor racial climate? Until recently, very few empirical studies had been done that could characterize the impact of a perceptual or attitudinal climate on students' development. A new literature has emerged on this issue, however. In terms of academic performance, students' general perceptions of discrimination have a significant and negative effect on African-American students' grades (Nettles

1988; Prillerman, Myers, and Smedley 1989; Smedley, Myers, and Harrell 1993). First-year students who reported being singled out or treated differently in the classroom were likely to have a higher sense of alienation at the end of their freshman year (Cabrera and Nora 1994). Although this finding was significant for all racial/ethnic groups, researchers found that this form of discrimination was particularly detrimental to African-American and other minority students in comparison with white students. A longitudinal study of Latino students attending a variety of four-year institutions found that perceptions of racial tension between groups on campus in the first year had a consistent negative impact across five dimensions of academic and psychological adjustment in the subsequent years of college (Hurtado, Carter, and Spuler 1996). The study also found that although reports of overt instances of personal harassment or discrimination did not significantly affect academic and personal-emotional adjustment, these overt acts tended to diminish Latino students' feelings of attachment with the institution.

A study of Native American students confirmed that perceptions of racial hostility were strongly associated with feelings of isolation, but the effect on attitudes toward college or grade point average was not decisively significant (Lin, LaCounte, and Elder 1988). Another study of college freshman found that perceptions of discrimination affected minority students' academic and social experiences on college campuses but did not directly affect their persistence in college (Nora and Cabrera 1996). It may be that some of the more academically confident students of color continue to feel marginalized in college but learn how to deal with instances of personal discrimination. This hypothesis appears to be supported by a study that found that an understanding and ability to deal with racism had a positive effect on the retention of upper-division African-American undergraduates (Tracey and Sedlacek 1985). Among students of color retained through graduation, however, campuses may also discover high levels of alienation: One study found less satisfaction and more social alienation among African-American and Asian-American students who were retained until the fourth year than their counterparts who opted to leave the university, presumably for better environments (Bennett and Okinaka 1990). These findings show that institutional attention to reports of discrimination and perceptions of hostility on campus is paramount to providing a welcoming and satisfying undergraduate experience. Introducing mechanisms for students to report and seek redress for these experiences is also important, but campuses must be aware that many aspects of the psychological dimension of the climate go unreported. For example, a study of California State institutions revealed that Asian Pacific–Americans often do not use formal grievance procedures when they experience discrimination or harassment (Asian Pacific 1994).

Research has begun to further distinguish among the sources and multiple effects of discrimination in college. Interviews of American Indian students revealed that although they perceived that non-Indian students were a major source of discrimination, students also encountered resentment and stereotyping from campus administrative staff with regard to the funding for Indians' higher education (Huffman 1991). Research using a variety of measures of racial climate found that the most significant measure of climate concerned black students' perceptions of racial discrimination on the part of college administrators. Both studies show that administrative staff, as a source of discrimination, can be a key contributor to a diminished sense of belonging among African-American and American Indian students attending predominantly white campuses. These results strongly suggest that administrators can shape the racial climate on their campuses and may unknowingly thwart students' success. The studies call for increased training in cultural sensitivity for administrators and underscore the importance of ensuring that campus policies treat all groups fairly. The same study of predominantly white campuses that had successfully achieved substantial enrollments of African-American students found that white students' sense of belonging was negatively affected by a perception of a poor racial climate but was positively tied to having nonwhite friends and perceptions that the campus accepts and respects African-American students (Gilliard 1996). Similarly, another study found that white students' persistence in college was directly and indirectly affected by perceptions of discrimination (Nora and Cabrera 1996). These studies show that the campus racial climate becomes important to white students' adjustment on campuses that have achieved some amount of success in diversifying their student bodies. In summary, the research suggests that the perceptions of a

. . . white students' sense of belonging was negatively affected by a perception of a poor racial climate . . .

discriminatory environment and poor relations among groups is not inconsequential for the success of students of color, and that it also is important for white students on campuses that have achieved relative success in diversifying their student bodies.

Development of Attitude and Reduction Of Prejudice in College

It is during the college years that students may exhibit greater openness to change in social and political attitudes. Researchers have indicated that late adolescence and early adulthood are the "impressionable years," a period during the life cycle when individuals may be particularly vulnerable to the formation of attitudes and change (Alwin, Cohen, and Newcomb 1991). Thus, students may be ready for opportunities that will result in the development of greater tolerance and acceptance of others from various racial and ethnic backgrounds. A revision of Chickering's seven vectors of development among college students places greater emphasis on tolerance and the appreciation of intercultural differences as an important part of the development of mature interpersonal relationships (Chickering and Reisser 1993). Both these major contributions to theories of student development suggest that colleges have the opportunity to affect change in students' attitudes through student peers, faculty influence, and structured education programs.

The influence of peers and reference groups

From the time we are toddlers all the way through adulthood, our peers play a critical role in our development and socialization. Research reveals that, because of our need to affiliate with or belong to particular groups, the formal and informal messages and expectations communicated by peers powerfully influence and shape our attitudes and behaviors. Peer groups in college are very influential and are responsible for much of the socialization and learning that occurs in the college and university environment. The following synthesis of the research may enable educators to create environments that are likely to become proactive forces in the socialization of college students toward greater tolerance of different groups.

Historically, social scientists have recognized the importance of the groups to which individuals belong in shaping the attitudes and behavior of people. The term "reference group" refers to the group toward which an individual orients himself or herself, regardless of whether or not the individual is actually a member of the group (Singer 1981). The development of the concept of reference groups drew attention to the idea that an individual's attitudes and behaviors may be shaped by groups different from the one considered to represent an individual's current affiliation. In other words, students are likely to modify their attitudes and beliefs to be consistent with those of groups to which they hope to belong.

An inherent assumption of one of the most widely cited definitions of college impact asserts that colleges and universities serve as agents of socialization for the larger society.

As socializing institutions, colleges and universities have the task of influencing students so that they leave the campus with improved or different knowledge, skills, attitudes, and values. Designated socializing agents (primarily the faculty) act on behalf of the organization to train, develop, modify, or in some way "act upon" the individuals (students) who enter it, in more or less formal ways (Feldman and Newcomb 1969, pp. 227–28).

Although faculty may be socializing agents, researchers believe that students and their peers are principally responsible for much of the socialization that transpires (Feldman and Newcomb 1969). More directly stated, "a student's most important teacher is another student" (Chickering 1969, p. 253). These points are not meant to minimize the role that faculty play. Rather, they suggest that the normative influence of faculty is frequently amplified or attenuated by the interaction students have with their peers. "The evidence clearly indicates that friends, reference groups, and the general student culture clearly have an impact on student development" (p. 269). "The force of friendships, reference groups, and the student culture is amplified as frequency and intensity of contacts increase" (p. 278).

To fully assess the role of peer groups in the personal development of college students, it is important to determine the conditions under which these groups function best. Four key conditions help to determine a peer group's influence:

size of the group, *homogeneity* of the group, *isolation* of the group, and *importance to individuals of group-supported attitudes* (Newcomb 1966). With regard to size, smaller groups tend to have stronger effects on individual attitudes (Newcomb 1966), although larger groups are also potentially effective, particularly when the smaller group is a subset of a larger or dominant group. If the attitudes held by the minority group are consistent with those of the dominant group, then the two may combine for a rather potent effect on an individual's attitudes. On the other hand, when the smaller group and its attitudes conflict with those of the dominant group, the smaller group can often serve to insulate its members from the effect of the dominant group norms. Hence, the relative isolation of a smaller peer group from other groups with different views and attitudes serves to strengthen the belief that the group's views are "right," frequently allowing the norms of the smaller group to remain intact. Generally speaking, groups that are more homogeneous in terms of age, sex, racial/ethnic background, social class, and/or religious beliefs contribute to the effective influence of peer groups primarily through the homogeneity of attitudes that tend to correspond with these characteristics. Simply put, people with similar backgrounds and experiences are more likely to share similar attitudes and ideas. Finally, the greater the importance attributed to the attitudes for which the group stands, the greater the solidarity of the group. Conversely, when identification of the individual shifts away from the group and its prevailing attitudes, the influence of the group on the individual's attitudes is diminished.

Astin's theory of the effects of peer groups includes psychological and sociological components that expand the theories of a peer group's influence. From the psychological perspective, peer groups are "a collection of individuals with whom the individual *identifies* and *affiliates* and from whom the individual seeks *acceptance* or *approval*" (Astin 1993, p. 400). According to Astin, identification is the recognition that other people are like one's self in certain key respects. In this schema, identification and affiliation go hand in hand with a student's need for acceptance and approval. From the sociological perspective, peer groups can be "any group of individuals in which the members identify, affiliate with, and seek acceptance and approval from each other" (p. 401). Acceptance in the sociological perspective refers to the

group's recognition that individuals have a certain set of characteristics that qualify them for membership in the group, which is also accompanied by a sense of how well the individual's values and behaviors conform to the expectations of the other group members.

Peer groups can effect change in students' attitudes with regard to perceived growth in cultural awareness and changes in personal commitment to promoting racial understanding during college. Six types of peer measures have had some effect on students' reports of growth in cultural awareness over four years. Characteristics of peer groups that had positive effects on cultural awareness include members who come from a high socioeconomic background, have higher levels of altruism or social activism, are more feminist in their orientation, are artistically inclined, or are more liberal in their political orientation (Astin 1993). Negative effects on students' attitudes came from peer groups whose members are more materialistic or focused more on status. Students' commitment to the goal of helping to promote racial understanding was influenced by four types of peer measures. Positive attitudinal effects were found for students with peers from higher socioeconomic backgrounds, higher levels of altruism and social activism, and higher levels of political liberalism. Similar to the results on cultural awareness, negative effects on commitment to this goal were found among students whose peers were more materialistic and focused on status.

The influence of faculty as a normative reference group

Studies of the impact of college on white students' racial attitudes, levels of cultural awareness and acceptance, and selected social and political attitudes (Milem 1992, 1994a, 1994b) are similar to Astin's findings (1993) about the impact of student peer groups. In addition to measures of the peer environment, these studies considered measures to assess the impact faculty norms might have on students' attitudes. Although students are widely believed to be the primary agents of socialization for their peers in colleges and universities, the research suggests that faculty may have a more important role as a referent group than has been traditionally hypothesized (Milem 1992, 1994a, 1994b). For example, faculty normative environments characterized as more materialistic in their orientation had negative effects on students' attitudes toward school busing and students' commitment to promoting racial understanding. On the other hand, faculty members' socially liberal views had positive effects on students' support for busing. Similarly, faculty normative groups that were more activist in their orientation were found to have positive effects on students' commitment to the personal goal of helping to promote racial understanding.

Hence, evidence shows that the attitudes and values of faculty on different campuses affect students' attitudes on those respective campuses. Although some contend that faculty are (or should be) "value free" and objective in their teaching and research, the findings of these studies suggest that the attitudes and values of faculty are reflected in their work and that these values influence the attitudes and values of their students. Given these findings, perhaps it would be in the best interests of our students to shift the discussion away from the dualistic proposition of whether or not faculty can (or should) be objective in their work and instead frame the discussion in a way that helps faculty understand how to become aware of their own attitudes and the effect of these attitudes on the students they teach.

Racial attitudes and the role of education, contact, and campus activities

One critical component in understanding racial attitudes is determining the role that education has in the formation and/or alteration of racial attitudes. It is generally assumed that higher levels of educational achievement correspond with greater open-mindedness with regard to racial attitudes (Schuman, Steeh, and Bobo 1985). Researchers suggest that the relationship between higher educational attainment and attitudes on racial issues is generally positive; however, they have found that income is negatively related to attitudes regarding support for racial policies, which tends to produce some rather conflicting findings, given that people with higher levels of education also tend to have higher incomes.

These findings lend support to other studies that show higher levels of education do not always indicate increased "progressiveness" in racial attitudes (Jackman 1978; Jackman and Muha 1984). Although those with higher levels of education tend to express more agreement with the abstract principles of equality, class interests override commitment to these principles. Thus, stated commitments to abstract principles of equality among educated individuals do not always translate into an increased likelihood that individuals will agree with statements that urge an applied or concrete implementation of these principles of equity.

Some researchers believe that whites' opposition to busing or affirmative action programs and policies is better explained through an understanding of group conflict theory (Bobo 1983; Kluegel and Bobo 1993). Group conflict theory holds that some individuals oppose these programs because they threaten the social status of whites. In short, white individuals view these policies as "a threat to their lifestyles, as well as other valued resources and accepted practices" (Bobo 1983, p. 1198). The resistance that white individuals express to these programs and policies does not necessarily reflect a rejection of African Americans as a group. Rather, this opposition is expressed in defense of "a lifestyle and position they think they have earned and do not question" (p. 1208). An analysis of data from the 1990 General Social Survey reports similar findings regarding the influence of a group's self-interest and perceived discrimination (Kluegel and Bobo 1993). Further, levels of self-interest, beliefs about inequality, and racial attitudes on issues differ based upon whether or not the policy in question is race-targeted, and the authors recommend that for optimal acceptance and support for policies, such initiatives should be defined as "opportunity enhancing" instead of "race-targeted" or "social welfare." These findings seem relevant to the higher education community in that they may help us to understand why institutions experience hostility with regard to the existence of minority-targeted programs and services. This research suggests that a real sense of "group" conflict may be motivating opposition to these programs and services, particularly in an era when many units face budgetary cuts.

A discussion of the effects of contact on racial attitudes (Allport 1954) is directly relevant to discussion of the impact of college on students' racial attitudes. Contact among groups can serve to lessen or to increase prejudice, depending on the nature and quality of the contact (Allport 1954). Six areas should be observed in examining the relationship between interracial contact and individual attitudes: (1) the quantitative aspects of contact (e.g., frequency, duration, number of people involved); (2) the status aspects of contact (inferior, equal, superior); (3) the role aspects of contact (competitive versus cooperative); (4) the social atmosphere involved in the contact (e.g., voluntary versus involuntary contact, important or intimate contact versus trivial or transient contact); (5) the personality of the people involved (e.g., how firmly rooted prejudice is); and (6) the area of contact (e.g., casual, residential, occupational). This research has served as the basis for many studies because of the clearly articulated nature of contact and conditions under which prejudice can be reduced.

Allport discusses different types of contact and their possible effects. *Casual contact* does not dispel prejudice and in fact is more likely to reinforce it. Moreover, he asserts, the prejudice varies with the density of the minority group or groups. The greater the level of casual contact in high-density situations, the more likely they are to bring negative results. *Acquaintance contact* in the sense of true acquaintance is more likely to lessen prejudice. Contacts that bring about knowledge and understanding are likely to bring about more accurate and stable beliefs about minority groups and, as a result, tend to contribute to the reduction of prejudice. *Residential contact* tends to operate on two different levels. For white individuals who live with blacks, prejudice is lessened (Allport 1954). This change does not happen merely by circumstance but rather as a result of increased communication. On the other hand, whites who view residential contact as an approaching phenomenon (as when they are about to be confronted with integrated living situations) see it as a threat and are very hesitant. Research indicates that the level of complaints varied according to the immediacy of the perceived threat.

For any of these types of contact to have a profound effect on attitudes, the contact must transcend casual acquaintance (Allport 1954). Contacts that facilitate the reduction of prejudice are those that cause people to do things together. Although the effects of contact cannot always overcome the effects of personal characteristics in prejudice, contact could lessen prejudice if any of three (and ideally all) of the following conditions are met: (1) equal status contacts occur between majority and minority groups in pursuit of common goals; (2) the effect is greatly enhanced if contact is sanctioned by institutional support; and (3) the contact is of the sort that leads to a perception of common interests and common humanity among members of the groups (Allport 1954).

Arguments for desegregation have been motivated in large part by the belief that greater levels of contact will produce positive changes in our society. More than 50 years ago, Gunnar Myrdal (1944) asserted that segregation was the primary factor responsible for the maintenance of cycles of discrimination, inferiority, and racial prejudice. This assertion has served as one of the essential arguments in efforts to desegregate our society and our educational system. In essence, it is believed that desegregation should provide for greater contact between people of different races and that this contact should decrease stereotyping and improve race relations. It is not clear, however, that this case is true in all situations. The findings on the effects of desegregation on racial prejudice appear to be inconclusive. Therefore, it is crucial that we develop an understanding of reasons for the conflicting outcomes resulting from studies of interracial contact that are the result of desegregation.

A study of a randomly stratified sample of black and white freshmen at a private, elite, urban university in the Midwest found that interracial contact did not lead to reduced prejudice among students (Sampson 1986). In fact, racial attitudes became increasingly negative over the course of the study, and the author suggests that these findings may have resulted because, at least in part, at least two (and possibly three) of Allport's conditions for positive change had not been met. First, the contact between students was not "prolonged," as Allport specified. Second, the contact that did occur was not likely to have been viewed by either blacks or whites as constituting equal status contact. Finally, because the contact took place in an "elite university setting," the contact was not likely to have occurred in a noncompetitive atmosphere, which is a stipulation that increases the potential of contact to reduce prejudice (Sampson 1986).

Research suggests that structured interaction is important for improving racial attitudes . . .

Research suggests that structured interaction is important for improving racial attitudes, including students' engaging in intensive forms of contact. The work of several researchers provides us with some clear direction (see, e.g., Hurtado 1990, 1992; Milem 1992, 1994a, 1994b; Springer, Palmer, Terenzini, Pascarella, and Nora 1996). Specifically, these studies show that a number of activities that students become involved in during college are positively related to students' commitment to the goal of helping to promote racial understanding and the willingness to have contact with others from a different racial/ethnic background. (Milem also examined students' support for school busing as well as changes in levels of students' cultural awareness and acceptance.) Socializing with someone of a different racial/ethnic group, discussing issues related to race and ethnicity, attending racial awareness workshops, enrolling in ethnic studies classes, and participating in campus demonstrations were positively related to changes in racial attitudes and commitment to improving racial understanding (Hurtado 1990, 1992; Milem 1992, 1994a, 1994b). Other studies confirm the importance of participation in racial and cultural awareness workshops to promote white students' willingness to learn about and have contact with others from a different racial/ethnic background (Springer et al. 1996). Moreover, time spent talking with faculty outside class, being a guest in a professor's home, and working in student organizations were also positive predictors of students' increased commitment to the goal of promoting racial understanding (Hurtado 1990). Membership in a fraternity or sorority was negatively related to increased commitment to this goal, however.

These findings show how particular peer group activities in college can facilitate or hinder a change in attitude with regard to racial and ethnic diversity. At the same time, however, the research suggests specific curricular and cocurricular activities that can be implemented on college campuses to improve students' knowledge and attitudes about different groups, and to increase understanding of differences across communities. The next section considers faculty practices and student activities that promote social interaction across race and ethnicity on college campuses and lead to important educational outcomes.

THE BEHAVIORAL DIMENSION OF THE
INSTITUTIONAL CLIMATE

Increasingly, campuses have been concerned with reports of racial incidents and the level of social interaction among different racial/ethnic groups (Farrell and Jones 1988; Loo and Rolison 1986). The behavioral dimension of the institutional climate consists of actual reports of general social interaction, interaction between and among individuals from different racial/ethnic backgrounds, and the nature of relations between and among groups on campus. Because students' involvement in campus life plays a central role in the successful educational experience of undergraduates, including the enhancement of cognitive and affective student outcomes (Astin 1988, 1991, 1993; Kuh, Schuh, Whitt, Andreas, Lyons, Strange, Krehbiel, and MacKay 1991) and retention (Tinto 1987, 1993), this section includes additional studies regarding students' involvement in campus activities, participation in student organizations, and use of specific types of campus programs. The focus is on a range of racial/ethnic diversity behaviors that constitute "integrating" student experiences.

Students' Involvement in College
And Intergroup Relations

An extensive review of the research regarding the impact of college on students speaks to the crucial role that involvement (with peers, faculty, and various institutional activities) has in educational attainment for all students (Pascarella and Terenzini 1991). "The environmental factors that maximize attainment include a cohesive peer environment (that is, students develop close on-campus friendships), frequent participation in college-sponsored activities, and a perception that the institution has a high level of personal involvement with and concern for the individual student" (p. 417). Moreover, the research suggests that both the increased involvement in extracurricular activities and the nature and quality of students' social interactions with peers and faculty have a positive influence on persistence, educational aspirations, completion of a bachelor's degree, and attendance at graduate school (Pascarella and Terenzini 1991).

This review of research regarding students' development of identity and self-esteem during college suggests that the most important influences that affect "academic and social self-images may flow from students' involvement in the formal and informal academic and social systems of their institution" (Pascarella and Terenzini 1991, p. 192). The formal systems referred to include classes, grades, cocurricular activities, rules and regulations, and so on. The informal systems are the regular interactions students have with other students and with faculty members, including the normative pressures that these groups exert as peer and normative reference groups. In addition to the research already reviewed that shows how participation in specific out-of-class and in-class activities is associated with attitudinal changes in students, a growing body of literature suggests that such activity is associated with increased interaction across races and improving the environment for students of color.

A series of studies now links students' involvement with enhanced social interaction across racial/ethnic groups on campus. A qualitative study of 15 colleges notes that institutions characterized as "involving colleges" have distinct characteristics (Kuh et al. 1991). Involving colleges foster high expectations for students' performance, minimize distinctions in status among individuals and groups in everyday practices (although status conventions are used to convey respect on some campuses), and, perhaps most important, have an unwavering commitment to multiculturalism. Other studies reveal links between involvement on campus and race relations. For example, campus race relations can significantly affect black students' involvement (Allen 1988); moreover, social factors (feelings of alienation and sources of social support) are more likely to affect the performance of African-American students who enroll at predominantly white institutions than their peers who attend HBCUs (Jackson and Swan 1991). The more often African-American males feel a part of campus life on predominantly white campuses, the better they tend to perform (Jackson and Swan 1991). Another study found that students who were involved in academics, socialize with other students, participate in an honors program, attend a racial cultural awareness workshop, participate in a racial/ethnic student organization, or play in intercollegiate sports tended to dine, study, room, or date someone of a different racial/ethnic group more frequently (Hurtado, Dey, and Treviño 1994). In sum, studies have shown that school-sponsored extracurricular activities can promote cross-race contact (E. Scott and Damico 1982).

An analysis of the impact that campus interpersonal relations and social networking have on students' academic performance, satisfaction with academic life, and occupational aspirations for African-American students who attend HBCUs and predominantly white institutions notes that these social support systems serve three important roles (R. Davis 1991). They provide for "(1) the maintenance of individual self-esteem and life satisfaction; (2) increasing social and academic competence and environmental mastery; and (3) the management of stress and coping" (p. 145).

Institutions exhibit distinct differences in the extent to which black students feel welcome and are willing to become involved in campus activities, however. Black students at white colleges were less likely to report that extracurricular activities on campus reflect their interests than were their peers at HBCUs (R. Davis 1991). This situation appears to have an effect on their rates of participation in campus life. Black students on white campuses were somewhat less likely to report that they are involved in campus clubs and organizations, although participation in student organizations was the best predictor of educational outcomes (R. Davis 1991). African-American students who participated in campus organizations at predominantly white institutions were less likely to report that they had considered dropping out of school and were more likely to report that they were more satisfied with campus life. The study also points out that it may be that students who attend predominantly white institutions are somewhat more likely to look to faculty for social support, which may be because African-American students on white campuses have fewer places to go to find peer social support than do their counterparts at HBCUs.

These results speak to the need for social support systems that serve to "buffer and/or solve academic difficulties and increase satisfaction with campus life" (R. Davis 1991, p. 157) and relate to findings on minority status stresses (Smedley, Myers, and Harrell 1993). Although certain experiences affect minority students that affect all students as part of the adjustment to college, minority students have unique experiences that contribute to their lower sense of "belonging and interfere with minority students' effective integration into the university community (for example, experiences with racism, questions about their right to be on campus)" (Smedley, Myers, and Harrell 1993, p. 435). These minority status stresses have both direct (as in overt prejudice or discrimination) and indirect effects on students. Indirect effects work by complicating and/or adding to the regular stressors experienced by all students and result from "the marginal social, political, and economic status of many minority students" (p. 436). The authors of the study tested whether or not these minority status stresses added to the difficulty of adjusting to college for minority students during their freshman year.

The authors found that chronic role strain (believed to be experienced by all students) is the main predictor of psychological distress, but they also found that a scale representing achievement stresses—characterized by the degree to which students doubted their ability to succeed in college, felt less intelligent or capable than their peers, felt that their academic preparation was inadequate, and/or felt some pressures from their families to succeed in college—was the one stress scale for minorities that served as a significant positive predictor of both psychological distress and freshman GPA. This finding should be viewed with some concern when we consider that the sample of African-American, Chicano/Latino, and Filipino students was drawn from a highly selective public university with a record of past academic achievement (including high scores on the SAT and high GPAs in high school).

More visible or overt forms of stress with regard to interracial conflict or experiences of overt racism or discrimination were not significant predictors of distress. Rather, "the more debilitating minority status stressors were those that undermined students' academic confidence and ability to bond to the university. These stresses [came] from both internal sources as well as from the demographic composition and social climate of the campus" (Smedley, Myers, and Harrell 1993, p. 448). The authors call for interventions that help students "to understand the interplay of the additional stresses they will face from their peers and from faculty [and provide] academic support services" (p. 449), and they recognize the need to alter aspects of the university environment in ways that will make campuses "less alien and more culturally and emotionally accessible to a diverse student population" (p. 448).

The Classroom Environment and Its Link with Social Interaction

A great deal has been written in recent years about the "chilly" classroom climate for women and students of color in higher education (see, e.g., Sandler and Hall 1982; Sedlacek and Brooks 1976; Trujillo 1986). These studies highlight the negative effect that faculty members' classroom behavior can have on students' learning experiences and self-esteem. Less emphasis, however, has been placed on the positive role that faculty might play in creating a more supportive climate for diversity on campus. Thus, the authors reviewed studies to gain a greater understanding of faculty behaviors and student activities that can enhance interaction across race and ethnicity in the classroom.

A review of 20 years of research on black students on white campuses states that one of seven noncognitive variables deemed important to the educational success of African-American students involves an ability to make a realistic self-appraisal as to how they are doing in school (Sedlacek 1987), but the research suggests that this appraisal is difficult for many African-American students on predominantly white campuses to achieve because faculty are less likely to provide these students with consistent reinforcement compared with white students. Moreover, studies indicate that African-American students consistently report feelings of prejudice directed at them by white faculty. The prejudice takes many forms, including "lower expectations of black students than are warranted, overly positive reactions to work quality, reducing the quality of communications, and reducing the probability that faculty know students well enough to write references" (p. 487).

A sentiment existing among some scholars in higher education suggests that competition, which is among one of the fundamental values of our society and our higher education system, is detrimental to many of our students, but particularly to students of color and women (see, e.g., Belenky, Clinchy, Goldberger, and Tarule 1986; Palmer 1987; Sandler 1987; Sandler and Hall 1982). In fact, the idea of competition (evidenced by grading on a curve and assigning individual rather than group-oriented projects) serves to perpetuate an elitist view of higher education that causes colleges and universities to focus on the acquisition of resources and engage in other behaviors that serve to further their academic "reputation." An institutional focus on resources and reputation is also related to perceptions of higher levels of campus racial conflict among white, African-American, and Chicano students (Hurtado 1992). This type of focus also frequently runs counter to a concern for and commitment to the learning of individual students (Astin 1985, 1991, 1993).

The idea of competition serves to perpetuate an elitist view of higher education that causes colleges and universities to focus on the acquisition of resources and engage in other behaviors that serve to further their academic "reputation."

An emerging body of work offers some clues as to what faculty can do to proactively promote interaction across race and ethnicity. An analysis comparing predictors of white and African-American students' achievement found that African-American students were likely to report higher GPAs when they reported higher levels of out-of-class contact with faculty, were exposed to faculty who used nontraditional teaching styles, and had faculty who reported higher levels of satisfaction with their jobs (Nettles 1991). Distressingly, African-American students are much less likely to have faculty who report high levels of out-of-class contact with students (Nettles 1991).

These findings complement those cited earlier (R. Davis 1991) suggesting that the role of faculty in the educational experience of African Americans on predominantly white campuses is particularly crucial (see also Haniff 1991). Moreover, they suggest that black students are likely to look to members of the faculty for the different types of support that are crucial to their success in college. Such relationships are related to students' feeling a sense of belonging to an institution as well as to their academic performance in class. Clearly, these "contacts, which are spontaneous or emanate from faculty who do genuinely care, *do* make a difference, and it is this contact and caring [that] combats racism" (Haniff 1991, p. 248).

Findings from studies of the campus racial climate (Hurtado 1992; Hurtado, Carter, and Sharp 1995) and the racial and social attitudes of college students (Milem 1992, 1994a, 1994b) reveal specific behaviors guided by instructors' pedagogical approaches that can influence students' attitudes. Students who reported that they had attended racial awareness workshops, had socialized with someone from another race, had more frequently discussed racial/ethnic issues, had more frequently discussed political and social issues, and/or had enrolled in ethnic studies courses were more likely to report more "liberal" or supportive attitudes toward race as well as greater relative levels of commitment to racial issues four years after they entered college. Clearly, if faculty are able to define course content in ways that touch on these issues and are able to employ pedagogical approaches that encourage students to engage in these activities in noncompetitive ways (i.e., cooperative and collaborative learning experiences, group projects, opportunities for prolonged cross-race interaction), they are likely to encourage their students to develop greater understanding and sensitivity to racial/ethnic diversity and social problems that confront our society.

In a study of social interaction among students from different self-perceived ability groupings, researchers identified tangible steps faculty can take to help create opportunities for students to interact across race/ethnicity and ability groupings (Hurtado, Carter, and Sharp 1995). Certain key academic involvements lead to students' more frequent informal socializing across race and ethnicity. For example, students who frequently study together are more likely to frequently interact with different racial and ethnic groups. Through pedagogical techniques, faculty can help to structure opportunities in the classroom that will promote relations and interactions across racial and ethnic groups; these "activities might include the development of topical study groups, requiring group projects as part of their evaluation of student work, or creating a community service component for their classroom material" (Hurtado, Carter, and Sharp 1995, p. 20). Other research has confirmed that cooperative learning activities, inside and outside the classroom, lead to intergroup friendships (Slavin 1985). When students are encouraged to come together to work cooperatively on course content, faculty provide them with the opportunity to learn more about each other as well as about specific content.

Faculty might also draw from approaches identified in postsecondary and K–12 research for guidance in developing curricular and pedagogical interventions that contribute to a more positive campus climate for diversity. A meta-analysis of research found that using role playing and antiracist teaching can reduce levels of prejudice in students (McGregor 1993). The degree of relative impact is greater for students in primary and secondary classrooms than it is for college and university students, but the effect is generally positive nonetheless. In addition, interracial interaction can be encouraged by aligning assignments with multicultural cocurricular activities on campus sponsored by student affairs. Specifically, more campuses are experimenting with three- to six-week and semester-length dialogue groups designed to encourage frank discussions among students about beliefs and stereotypes. These dialogues are guided by trained facilitators and are offered as one-credit classes or are conducted in conjunction with courses in education, sociology, and psychology. Research on this activity indicates that student interaction goes through several phases. Activities for the learning process include the opportunity to break down barriers, challenge the ignorance inside and outside oneself, create new insights, forge new connections and identities, and build coalitions to work toward a common goal (Zúñiga and Nagda 1992). The issues of group conflict and social attitudes surrounding communities of difference addressed in the dialogue groups are "not easily resolvable as long as the lack of adequate structures and processes for intergroup interactions in the college community maintains the invisible, but psychologically real walls that separate different groups" (p. 251). The creation of dialogue groups provides both a structure and process for addressing the intergroup dynamics of multiculturalism within the learning environment.

In addition to bringing students together in activities that lead to more hospitable campus climates, collaborative and cooperative approaches to learning in standard courses can positively affect students' learning and achievement. Treisman's work (1992) in the area of mathematics education is just one illustration of this point. Based in part on observations during work as a teaching assistant for calculus courses at the University of California at Berkeley, Treisman developed an approach to teaching college calculus that relies heavily on collaborative and cooperative learning techniques as well as on techniques used to build students' self-esteem. Observations of African-American students and Chinese-American students at Berkeley led Treisman to question why many African-American students tended to perform poorly in calculus while many Chinese-American students tended to do well; he found that the Chinese-American students tended to study and do homework in collaborative and cooperative work groups, while African-American students tended to work alone. Treisman decided to teach the course in a manner that would encourage African-American students to work together while at the same time engage them in activities that increase their efficacy for successfully doing calculus and, in turn, increase their self-esteem. This approach produced groups of students that excelled in calculus who previously had had difficulty in precalculus classes; it exemplifies one way to build proactively on the strengths of communities of cultural difference and tailor teaching in a multicultural campus environment.

Approaches to Curricular Change
And Diversity in the Classroom

Today's "students must learn, in every part of their educational experience, to live creatively with the multiplicity, ambiguity, and irreducible differences that are the defining conditions of the contemporary world" (Association 1995, p. xxii). One way that colleges have begun to ensure that this type of learning occurs has been through improved college curricula. In the last two decades, hundreds of colleges and universities have expanded their traditional conception of undergraduate liberal education as "intended to break down the narrow certainties and provincial vision with which we are born" (Association 1985, p. 22). These initiatives to improve diversity in the classroom have resulted in new multicultural education requirements in general education at more than one-third of all colleges, expanded curricular offerings at 50 to 75 percent of four-year colleges (Levine and Cureton 1992), and increased course activities designed to teach students about the multiple cultural legacies of our society and about issues of equity that both challenge and reinforce basic democratic principles and notions about justice.

Institutions can make a difference in terms of increasing multicultural competencies among students by influencing students' course-taking behaviors to ensure that they are exposed to readings and activities that help them understand what it means to live in a diverse society. This change cannot occur, however, without concerted changes in the content and pedagogy of the courses faculty teach. This subsection summarizes two different approaches taken by faculty who have worked to incorporate issues of racial and ethnic diversity into the curriculum. The first involves the planning and implementation of a course that is specifically designed to address issues of race and diversity. This approach to curricular change may be helpful to faculty who are interested in developing a course or courses that are meant to fill a current void in the curriculum in their department or at their institution. (See Tatum 1992 for a description of one model that should be considered when planning these courses and linking students' cognitive and affective development in the classroom.)

The second approach to curricular change is one in which issues of diversity are incorporated into the content of courses that are part of the existing core curriculum. This approach may be helpful to faculty who are interested in engaging in a

---

process of curricular transformation in their department and/or at their institution. Such efforts have had a positive effect on a sample of students involved in the study of human development at their institution (MacPhee, Kreutzer, and Fritz 1994). Both approaches confirm other studies that reveal students acquire cognitively complex skills and cultural understanding through content and pedagogy designed to make the most of the diversity in the classroom (Adams and Zhou-McGovern 1994; Ortiz 1995; Smith and Associates 1997).

As colleges and universities struggle to develop more courses that address issues of cultural representation within the curriculum, not enough attention is paid to "issues of process that inevitably emerge in the classroom when attention is focused on race, class, and/or gender" (Tatum 1992, p. 1). To really do justice to these topics, issues of racism, classism, and sexism must be addressed (Tatum 1992). This approach has one possible shortcoming, however. Given that efforts to address these issues are likely to generate powerful emotional reactions in students, they "can result in student resistance to oppression-related content areas" if not addressed in the classroom (p. 2). A description of the evolution of the instructor's approach to teaching for a course called Psychology of Racism offers "a framework for understanding students' psychological responses to race-related content and the student resistance that can result" (p. 2). Moreover, the description suggests strategies for helping students to overcome this resistance. Assuming that racism is pervasive in the socialization process in the United States, Tatum offers a set of working assumptions that underpin teaching in this area. She draws a clear distinction between prejudice (a preconceived judgment or opinion, often based on limited information) and racism (a system of advantage based on race). This distinction is important in identifying differences in power between members of dominant and subordinate groups. Racism is assumed to clearly work to benefit whites as a group in our society. Given that racism is such an intricate part of our socialization in the United States, Tatum assumes that people cannot be blamed for learning what they were previously taught but that, once people recognize that they have been misinformed, they have a responsibility to seek more accurate information and to behave accordingly. Moreover, Tatum assumes that change is possible for individuals and institutions.

An instructor frequently encounters several major sources of resistance when trying to teach students about issues of race and racism. Many students consider race a taboo topic for discussion, especially when they find themselves in racially mixed settings. Many students also believe "that the United States is a just society, a meritocracy where individual efforts are fairly rewarded" (Tatum 1992, p. 6). Students may also deny that they have any personal connection to racism. As a means for dealing with this anticipated resistance, Tatum offers strategies for reducing the likelihood that students will resist certain activities in the classroom: creating a safe classroom environment by establishing clear guidelines for discussion, creating opportunities for self-generated knowledge, providing a developmental model that students can use as a means for understanding their own process of identity as well as that of their peers (in this case the process of racial identity development described in Cross 1971, 1978, 1991; Cross, Parham, and Helms 1991; Helms 1990; Parham 1989), and exploring ways that will empower students as change agents. It is impossible for us to have "multiracial campuses without talking about race and learning about racism" (Tatum 1992, p. 23). The model described provides a means for this exchange to happen throughout the semester, as opposed to traditional workshops that meet with mixed success because they rely upon an evening, a day, or a weekend and are not as conducive to the growth and development of individuals or the class as a whole.

Other researchers provide important information for faculty interested in infusing the perspectives of racially/ethnically diverse populations into an already existing curriculum (MacPhee, Kreutzer, and Fritz 1994). The authors analyzed content of published research results in human development pertaining specifically to children and adolescents, and the descriptions of study samples to determine how frequently low-income and culturally diverse groups were included in studies. They also examined the "results" section of each article to determine whether or not data had been analyzed by income level, ethnicity, and the interaction between the two. Information regarding the family background was absent from a significant number of the studies (MacPhee, Kreutzer, and Fritz 1994). Further, fewer than one-third of the studies contained subjects from low-income or ethnically diverse backgrounds, and only half of those studies that did include representatives from these groups analyzed the data with regard to the ethnicity of the subject. The findings indicate that youth from low-income backgrounds were less likely to be included in studies of any kind but especially studies on "normative development," and that people of color were much more likely to be included in a study sample if the study focused on a social problem.

Based on these findings, the authors suggest a series of problems that this approach presents for pedagogy in their field. It is extremely difficult to present accurate and informative findings about ethnic and cultural differences in human development when this information is limited or nonexistent (MacPhee, Kreutzer, and Fritz 1994). Moreover, unless these studies successfully disentangle the effects of social class and ethnicity, biased stereotypes are likely to be perpetuated. "The confounding of race and social class exaggerates group differences because minorities are overrepresented in lower social strata . . . and are more likely to be drawn from clinical groups or captive inner-city sites that differ markedly from the more typical environments of adolescents" (p. 704). These improper comparative studies tend to perpetuate bigoted stereotypes by reinforcing perceptions of minorities as deviant, and many studies of adolescent development contain such a perspective of people of color.

A second study sought to determine the impact of efforts by faculty volunteers to "infuse multicultural content" into the courses of eight departments in the College of Applied Human Sciences. "The purpose was to promote cultural pluralism and social equality by using instructional materials that are appropriate for diverse students and that are integrated rather than supplementary" (MacPhee, Kreutzer, and Fritz 1994, p. 705). The efforts by faculty were coordinated to modify a specific sequence of courses, based on three reasons for the importance of this sequencing of classes. First, this effort conveys to students that the information is essential to their understanding of human behavior. Second, repeated exposure to this information is likely to reinforce these important lessons. Third, by making these issues central to the curriculum of human development, minority students are less likely to feel marginalized and stigmatized, which is likely to increase their identification with their profession.

In planning these courses, faculty worked to point out the deficiencies in the research literature discussed in the article by MacPhee, Kreutzer, and Fritz. Moreover, each course sought to use pedagogical approaches that promote critical thinking and are known to be effective with various styles of learning, including extensive use of cooperative learning, simulations (or problem-based learning), and cognitive dissonance as a means of identifying and changing incongruous beliefs.

The authors employed both qualitative and quantitative research methods during this phase of the study. The findings of the quantitative analyses suggest that students' attitudes toward "outgroups" (particularly the poor) were broadly influenced by the transformation of the curriculum. They also found small but statistically significant changes in students' racial attitudes. The qualitative analyses reveal three primary findings. First, students appeared to have mastered a number of critical thinking skills. Second, levels of ethnocentrism among students appeared to have declined. Third, students were consistently able to distinguish between poverty and ethnicity as developmental risk factors. These important curricular outcomes are all tied to careful thought in course planning and pedagogical approaches to diversifying the curriculum.

Campus Race Relations and Social Interaction

The prevailing view is that campus race relations are poor, social interaction is low, and we have witnessed a resurgence of segregation on college campuses among minority groups (Altbach and Lomotey 1991; Bunzel 1992). To be sure, incidents of overt racism and harassment occurred with greater frequently near the end of the 1980s and received much press coverage (Farrell and Jones 1988). A series of systematic research studies, however, has begun to present a different picture that reflects students' actual reports of interactions and relations on campus (Duster 1993; Hurtado, Dey, and Treviño 1994; Weiner 1992). Moreover, the view of whether or not groups are interacting with each other depends on one's standing as "insider" or "outsider." For example, although they may view "sameness" and "self-segregation" among minority groups, outside observers may be less attuned to differences within groups such as Latinos and Asian Pacific–Americans, who are attempting to forge common communities out of diverse backgrounds, ethnicities, and political experiences (Duster 1993). In another example, researchers found that white students interpreted ethnic group clustering as racial segregation, whereas minority students tended to view this behavior as a method of cultural support within a larger unsupportive environment (Loo and Rolison 1986). The following analysis of recent studies presents an emerging portrait of relations in a multicultural context.

In 1991, college students at 390 institutions were surveyed about the frequency with which they dined, roomed, socialized, or dated someone from a racial/ethnic group different from their own (Hurtado, Dey, and Treviño 1994). Chicano, Asian-American, and African-American students reported widespread and frequent interaction across race/ethnicity in these informal situations, while white students were least likely to report engaging in any of the activities across race. Earlier studies focusing on black and white interracial contact confirmed the fact that black students were significantly more likely to report having close friends of another race than were white students (Minatoya and Sedlacek 1980). Although it is clear that racial/ethnic groups are more likely to engage in interaction across race precisely because they are a minority on predominantly white campuses, this fact seems to be ignored by "outsiders" who observe these students interacting with someone from their own racial/ethnic group on campus. Further multivariate analysis shows that higher black and Hispanic enrollments did not significantly affect interaction across ethnicity for white students but that higher Asian enrollments had a positive impact (Hurtado, Dey, and Treviño 1994). This finding suggests that variations in the structural diversity result in variations in social interaction, but these effects appear to be different for each racial/ethnic group.

Students were also surveyed about the extent to which they have felt excluded or harassed because of their racial/ethnic background. Among the groups, African Americans and Asian Pacific–Americans were most likely to report such instances of harassment (32 percent and 30 percent, respectively). Such experiences did not significantly diminish interaction across race/ethnicity for these groups, however. Thus, even in the face of overt discrimination, some groups continue to interact across race/ethnicity.

A review of institutional self-studies of race relations among students at four West Coast campuses confirms many of these patterns of interaction across race for white and racial/ethnic minority groups (Weiner 1992). At the same time, the review found that more interaction occurred across racial/ethnic groups than the national media would have us believe. For race and ethnic relations to improve, we need not only more friendship among students, but also more knowledge about the economics, politics, and sociology of race relations, more discussions of attitudes and practices that affect race relations, and more group projects to encourage people to work together across ethnic lines. Colleges and universities, and especially their faculties, have an opportunity to "build on the receptivity of students to interethnic understanding and cooperation" (p. 11). We have neglected to see some of the good news coming out of campus studies suggesting that interaction is actually occurring and that higher education can build on this potential through its educational mission (Weiner 1992).

What prevents more social interaction across race and ethnicity on campus? First, although researchers and campus administrators attempt to observe rates of cross-race and interethnic interaction on campus and to draw conclusions from the observations, we sometimes forget that "interaction between the races may have been nurtured long before these various students came to this institution" (Asante and Al-Deen 1984, p. 514). Approximately 83 percent of first-time, full-time entering college students in 1990 came from neighborhoods that are completely or mostly all white, and only 6.4 percent reported their neighborhoods were half white or nonwhite (Astin, Korn, and Berz 1991). It may be that some students are becoming accustomed to functioning in a diverse environment for the first time in college and that administrators need to remain sensitive to this issue. Second, dynamics among peer groups may hinder interaction. A case study of early adolescent peer groups revealed that loosely knit peer groups encourage interracial interaction, while cliques do not (Zisman and Wilson 1992). This finding attests to the influence of particular peer groups and their ability to manage boundaries intended to create "in groups" and "out groups." For example, the selection process and determination of group membership has largely gone unquestioned for peer organizations such as fraternities and sororities (Duster 1993). Administrators need to allow individual students to naturally form their own peer groups and to work with some of the formal student organizations to ensure that they remain open to all students and promote interaction across groups. Third, intergroup contact is influenced by an individual's psychological state, feelings of inadequacy, and comfort with and conceptions about the "other."

A study of Asian-American and Hispanic college students, for example, reveals that low levels of intergroup contact with Caucasians were evident among students who had high levels of intergroup anxiety. High levels of intergroup anxiety or social awkwardness were associated with a preference for one's own group, the relative status of one's group, and stereotyping (Stephan and Stephan 1985). Such findings are thought to hold true for white students as well. Self-perceptions of ability in comparison with one's peers are also clear indicators of rates of social interaction. Students who rated themselves as "high ability" at college entry tended to interact more frequently across race/ethnicity and to participate in more activities on campus than students who rated themselves lower in ability compared with students their own age (Hurtado, Carter, and Sharp 1995). This finding suggests that the institution should do more to increase students' academic self-confidence, and willingness to take risks and cross racial/ethnic group boundaries in informal and formal social settings. Most important, institutions must provide support structures that allow students to develop both their academic skills and confidence so that they can become full participants in campus life.

Contact with Diverse Peer Groups
And Educational Outcomes

Research shows that interracial contact clearly influences students' views toward others, their support for campus initiatives, and important educational outcomes. One study found that white students who had the least social interaction with someone of a different background were less likely to hold positive attitudes toward multiculturalism on campus (Globetti, Globetti, Brown, and Smith 1993). "In order to prepare students as participants in a more heterogeneous college environment, and as citizens in a global community, program planners and administrators need to recognize deficiencies in cultural sensitivity and build on the multicultural awareness that students do have" (p. 218). Another study revealed that socializing across race and discussing racial/ethnic issues have a positive effect on students' retention, overall satisfaction with college, intellectual self-concept, and social self-concept (Chang 1996). Further, positive interracial contacts on campus lead to less difficulty in African-Americans' transition to college, which in turn is related to higher college GPAs and less intent to drop out of college (Bennett 1984). The complex dynamics of interaction on the University of California–Berkeley campus, where dramatic changes in racial/ethnic enrollments have occurred, suggest continued support for strong ethnic identities and affiliations as well as institutional encouragement for multiracial contacts (Duster 1993).

Numerous studies conducted in the last decade have established a clear and consistent effect of contact with diverse peers on educational outcomes. Studies emerging from the National Study of Student Learning reveal that students' openness to diverse perspectives and willingness to be challenged are significantly associated with a variety of intergroup contacts that include living in residence halls, participation in a racial cultural awareness workshop, and association with peers who are diverse in terms of race, interests, and values. Such effects in students' cognitive thinking were evident after the first year of college (Pascarella, Edison, Nora, Hagedorn, and Terenzini 1996) as well as in the second and third years of college (Whitt, Edison, Pascarella, Terenzini, and Nora 1998). These studies also confirm the importance of the psychological climate: A nondiscriminatory environment was conducive to students' openness to diverse perspectives and willingness to be challenged. In contrast, the homogeneity of one's college peers as measured by participation in a sorority or fraternity was negatively associated with this measure of cognitive complexity (Pascarella, Whitt, Nora, Edison, Hagedorn, and Terenzini 1996). A different national sample of students found that students who studied frequently with someone from a different racial/ethnic background reported growth on such learning outcomes as problem-solving skills, critical thinking, and ability to work cooperatively (Hurtado 1997). Stronger effects were evident on civic engagement outcomes that include cultural awareness, acceptance of people from different races/cultures, tolerance of different beliefs, and leadership ability. A third national study extends these findings: Students with a high proportion of diverse close friends reported growth in leadership and cultural knowledge and understanding after four years of college (Antonio 1998b). It is evident from these three national studies of college students that diverse peers are important factors in the learning environment and key educational outcomes related to skills for living in a complex, pluralistic society.

Participation in Racial/Ethnic Student Organizations And Minority Support Programs

"Campus support systems may be seen as transactions among students, professors, and staff [that] are indicators of participation and integration into campus life" (R. Davis 1991, p. 145). Racially and ethnically focused extracurricular and curricular activities have played a significant role in increasing students' participation in campus life and creating social support for various nonwhite racial and ethnic groups. Although some suggest that racial/ethnic student organizations and minority programs contribute to segregation on campus, a series of studies refutes this perspective. Studies have empirically demonstrated that students who join such racial/ethnic student organizations join them because they enhance identity and that such increased comfort with one's identity may lead to a greater interest in cultural and cross-cultural activities (Mitchell and Dell 1992; Treviño 1992). For example, members of racial/ethnic student organizations in one study were more likely to participate in racial/cultural awareness workshops (Treviño 1992). Students in such organizations also report more frequent interactions across race/ethnicity in informal situations (Hurtado, Dey, and Treviño 1994). Participation in racially focused cultural activities and support programs (for example, the Black Student Union or minority peer support services) was correlated with African-Americans' higher social involvement, informal social interactions with faculty, and higher use of general support services (Gilliard 1996). It may be that such programs and activities are part of a larger safety net that encourages students to take advantage of many of the other services and activities a college offers. In the absence of such programs, it is not clear whether minority students would take advantage of some of the "mainstream" services or have opportunities for leadership in typical college activities.

LINKING THE INSTITUTIONAL CLIMATE FOR DIVERSITY WITH THE GENERAL LEARNING ENVIRONMENT

This section reviews some general findings that have important implications for institutional practices that focus on students' academic and social development. These findings specifically relate to institutional priorities and emphases that have an important impact on student outcomes and the context for learning and socializing. For example, a key issue that has emerged from the literature is the extent to which students feel valued and validated in the environment. One study found that African-American, Chicano, and white students perceived lower racial tension on campuses that they perceived were "student-centered" (Hurtado 1992). Student-centeredness refers to the degree to which faculty and administrators convey an interest in students' academic and personal development. Racial conflict is greater on less student-centered campuses because a feeling persists that one group receives more attention than another, when really the quality of undergraduate education has declined for all students. Recent research on the transition of students from high school to college has also revealed the importance of receiving "validating experiences"—a series of in- and out-of-class experiences with family, faculty, and staff (Terenzini, Rendón, Upcraft, Millar, Allison, Gregg, and Jalomo 1994). These experiences convey the message that students are accepted and welcome in the college community, they can be successful, previous work and life experience are legitimate forms of knowledge, and their contributions in the classroom are valuable. In addition, a qualitative study of student life at a large university suggests that racial/ethnic minority students feel like a "guest" in someone else's house (Turner 1994). The study and additional work (Turner 1997) recommend transformation of the institution's core mission and values to create a welcoming environment for diverse students. These works suggest that the general environment of the campus must be accepting and convey the notion that all students are valued. Further, service to a diverse student population must become more central to the day-to-day practices and activities geared toward students' learning and development.

Perhaps one of the most important questions for colleges is what the outcomes are of a greater institutional emphasis on diversity for all students. *What Matters in College* (Astin 1993) describes a number of findings relevant to this question. Peer groups exert different influences on white and African-American students; specifically, white students tend to become more politically conservative after four years, while African-American students tend to become more politically liberal. In addition, whites and African Americans view racial issues differently in that they grow farther apart in their level of agreement with the statement "racial discrimination is no longer a major problem" and in their personal commitment to the goal of promoting racial understanding. "The college experience, rather than narrowing political differences between the two major racial groups in this country, actually serves to exacerbate already existing differences observed at the point of college entry" (Astin 1993, p. 407).

Whether or not these findings are viewed as matters of concern or optimism depends largely on whether or not an institution focuses on diversity as part of its educational mission. Although the aggregate data suggest how the two racial groups grow farther apart, differences exist in the extent to which cultural gaps and achievement outcomes occur on specific campuses. Further findings in this study indicate that institutions can narrow these gaps and enhance student outcomes by making diversity a high institutional priority. At least three measures of institutional emphasis on diversity, derived from student and faculty perspectives, are used in the study. *Diversity Emphasis* refers to the extent to which faculty at an institution believe that their institution is committed to issues of diversity and multiculturalism. *Faculty Diversity Emphasis* represents the extent to which faculty incorporate issues of race and gender into their teaching and/or scholarship. And *Diversity Orientation* is a scale made up of students' views of both these dimensions.

After controlling for the effects of various background characteristics of students and a wide range of environmental influences, the institution's Diversity Emphasis was shown to be positively correlated with increased levels of cultural awareness among students and increases in students' commitment to the goal of helping to promote racial understanding during college. Diversity Emphasis was also shown to be positively correlated with a variety of measures of satisfaction, including overall satisfaction, satisfaction with student life, opportunities to enroll in interdisciplinary courses, and overall quality of instruction. Conversely, this variable had a negative effect on students' belief that racial discrimination is no longer a problem in this country, on the likelihood that a student would join a fraternity or sorority or get married while in college, and on the belief that the chief benefit of attending college is to increase one's earning power. Thus, Diversity Emphasis tends to diminish students' tendencies to deny discrimination, join exclusive campus organizations, or seek an education purely for one's own financial benefit.

Faculty Diversity Emphasis, in terms of the curriculum, produces effects not unlike those found for the institutional Diversity Emphasis. Faculty Diversity Emphasis produced its greatest effects on students' cultural awareness and on overall satisfaction with the college experience. In addition, it increased the likelihood that a student would participate in civic duties (for example, voting in a presidential election). In this respect, learning about diversity and participation in our democracy are linked. Perhaps most important, students' perceptions of their college's orientation toward diversity in the curriculum and institutional priorities were negatively associated with reports of students' leaving college or transferring to a different college—suggesting that student retention rates can be enhanced when an institution communicates an emphasis on diversity. Generally speaking, this extensive longitudinal study of college students demonstrates that emphasizing diversity on college campuses tends to have consistently positive effects on students' undergraduate experiences (Astin 1993). At many levels, incorporating diversity as a central part of the institutional mission and a college's teaching and learning activities can happen, particularly with the support of state policy makers.

The Role of State Policy Makers in Promoting an Institutional Climate for Diversity

The focus of state policy on education has shifted over the last decades, from resistance to equity before the 1954 *Brown* decision, to mandated desegregation in elementary and secondary schools and a focus on removing barriers to a school's success in the 1960s and 1970s, to a concern about the overall quality of education in the 1980s (Matthews 1996). Although states have always maintained education as part of their responsibility, the federal government had assumed a good deal of responsibility for providing leadership for public policy to promote equity in education. The 1980s can be characterized as a transition from the federal government's providing leadership in policies for educational improvement to the states' assuming the mantle of leadership for policy in education reform (Callan 1994). This transition presents a bit of irony when we consider that "historically, the states have been perceived as the problem, and discussions of the state role still evoke the image of the governor blocking the schoolhouse door" (p. 336). This role is now clearly the responsibility of the states, and as the 1990s approached, greater attention to addressing the educational issues of African-American, Latino, and American Indian youth was evident in state reports addressing improvement in undergraduate education (Callan and Finney 1988).

States became increasingly aware of demographic shifts and were concerned about remaining economically competitive as we approached the 1990s (Matthews 1996). It is clearly in the economic interest of the states, and businesses within the states, to have a skilled labor force. The need to close the gaps between achievement for historically underrepresented groups and other students became apparent, and state policy makers have begun to initiate efforts to facilitate students' movement through the educational pipeline, improve undergraduate education, and improve requisite skills for a changing workplace with attainment of a baccalaureate degree. State higher education policies can provide the necessary infrastructure through funding, introduction of new programs, and reforms that require changes in public systems of higher education.

For these reasons, improving the quality of undergraduate experiences in state-funded colleges and universities has been present in many state policy reports since the late 1980s, with particular attention paid to participation and achievement of minority students. A report by the State Higher Education Executive Officers (SHEEO) calling attention to the need to improve equity, access, and achievement in public higher education received widespread attention (State 1987), and several states (California, Ohio, and Arizona) issued major reports on the participation and achievement of minorities (Callan and Finney 1988). The SHEEO Task Force on Minority Achievement (State 1987) offered several recommendations to respond to concerns about equity and achievement in higher education. Although the task force acknowledged the importance of maintaining a federal role in dealing with these issues, it recommended that states step forward to assume a key leadership role in responding to these issues. Among the recommendations, the task force reported that state higher education executive officers need to establish minorities' achievement as a preeminent concern for the higher education community in their states. Once their achievement is established as a top priority, state officers should put into place a formal institutional planning and reporting process, regularly disseminate the information to the public about opportunities in higher education for minority students, and report progress in meeting the needs of minority students. As for programming and funding, the task force urged states to creatively seek resources to support minority-related programming, aggressively involve K–12 education, and support institutional programming that will meet two equally important ends: to better equip students to function well in the institutional environment, and to adapt that environment to better accommodate the needs and interests of diverse students.

The National Task Force for Minority Achievement in Higher Education (1990) sponsored by the Education Commission of the States also offered a series of recommendations regarding the role of the states in achieving diversity on college and university campuses. That task force recommended that every state should embrace and work to achieve two goals: *equitable representation* in terms of enrollment proportional to the population in the state, and *comparable graduation rates* across all student groups. The task force suggested, based on its analyses of the differences between institutions that had successfully changed to achieve diversity and those that had not, that institutions should pass through a three-stage process of change. The first stage involves removing barriers to participation, the second helping students to achieve, and the third using "assessment, learning assistance, better teaching strategies, and curricular reform to change learning environments for all students" (p. 5). According to the task force, few institutions ever make it to stage three.

The task force offered suggestions for institutions as well as for state policy makers to help achieve the two recommended goals. Improved leadership on this issue could be demonstrated by establishing measurable goals, linking institutional funding to statewide goals for minority participation and achievement, and diversifying governing board members to reflect the state's diverse population. The removal of barriers to participation, stage one, hinged on improving financial aid programs to streamline the process and offset increases in tuition. Helping students to achieve, stage two, could be facilitated by statewide programs to ensure that every junior high and high school student is advised about and prepared for higher education. This stage is also facilitated by improving the articulation of transfer students to complete a baccalaureate degree in the same amount of time as other students. Improving undergraduate teaching and learning, stage three, addresses systemic reform in the core mission of institutions to address diversity. The task force's recommendations for this important stage include directives to:

- Fund basic skills assessments and programs that help students correct deficiencies;
- Require colleges and universities to use student assessment results to improve teaching and learning;
- Make teaching effectiveness a criterion for how state resources are allocated to institutions;
- Support and fund programs to recruit more minority faculty;
- Fund innovative approaches that integrate multicultural perspectives into the curriculum;
- Promote faculty and student exchanges and partnerships between historically black and predominantly white colleges and universities (National 1990, p. 16).

In essence, the recommendations for this last stage suggest overall changes in the campus environment and the core institutional mission that will ultimately achieve both quality and diversity in the educational experience.

Still other state reports directly address issues related to the climate for diversity. For example, in an effort to address the uneven success of students of color and women, the California Postsecondary Education Commission examined the feasibility of developing an educational equity assessment system to provide information on perceptions of the climate in the state's postsecondary institutions (California 1990). This effort was in part a response to legislation that asked the commission to examine factors that "contribute [to] or detract from an equitable and high-quality experience, particularly for women and students from historically underrepresented groups" (California 1990, p. 2), with an emphasis on the perceived level of equity in students' educational experiences. Thus, the legislators were distinctly interested in the psychological climate for diversity on college campuses. The directive for the study coincided with the commission's developing interest in understanding the quality of educational environments with respect to educational equity.

In another example, the state of Washington's Higher Education Coordinating Board issued a policy statement on minority participation and diversity in 1991. The policy was established "to achieve equitable levels of [college] participation for people of color, and to create higher education environments in which diversity is valued and promoted" (Washington 1991, p. 1). The policy established statewide goals for enrollment, retention, completion, employment, and institutional climate. The goals for climate included the development of a statement on valuing diversity and a timetable for introducing material on cultural pluralism and racism in American society across the undergraduate curriculum, continued participation of campus and faculty leaders in policy seminars for valuing and managing diversity, and development and implementation of workshops for staff, faculty, and students to combat racism and foster diversity.

Improving the campus climate has now become a matter of discussion at statehouses, and state higher education policy makers can do their part to improve human relations on campus (Marcus and Yavorsky 1989). Responses to campus racial/ethnic tensions generally occur as one of two types: incident-focused responses and climate-focused responses. *Incident-focused responses* are basically reactive in nature and tend to deal with symptoms. They tend to be "reactive rather than preventive, and [are] generally aimed at only the most obvious and flagrant forms of prejudicial behavior" (p. 3). Included in this type of response is the development of antiharassment policies. On the other hand, *climate-focused responses* are viewed as being more proactive in nature in that they focus more on what are believed to be the causes of the problem. These responses by the states seek "to identify the roots of the problem and implement a systematic action plan that is directly responsive to those identified concerns" (p. 3). It is a two-stage process that first mobilizes the interest and the motivation to take action at the institutional level, and second involves "facilitating, and in some cases directly mounting, the programs that are needed to bring about constructive change" (p. 3).

Although some state policy analysts have called for programmatic changes that directly address issues of the cam-

*The
Education
Commission
of the States
released a
policy guide
for leaders
to develop
and revise
action plans
aimed at
improving
learning
environ-
ments for
diverse
students.*

pus climate, others recommend that such approaches begin with systematic self-assessment (Richardson, Matthews, and Finney 1992). The Education Commission of the States released a policy guide for leaders to develop and revise action plans aimed at improving learning environments for diverse students. The guide suggests that state policy and institutional strategies improve the participation of diverse students in college, help students achieve, and ultimately focus on improving the learning environment (Richardson, Matthews, and Finney 1992). Congruent with these stages are state policies that address setting priorities, initiating programs, engaging in strategic planning to achieve quality and diversity, and ensuring the consistency of state policy across actors at various levels of authority and over a sustained period of time (Matthews 1996). The guide asks specific questions to assist policy makers in assessing aspects of each stage, including important questions about creating a comfortable climate for all students.

Although not all states have developed plans to directly assess or improve the climate, several studies have identified a variety of state policy initiatives aimed at improving the achievement and participation of underrepresented students (Callan 1988; Matthews 1996; State 1987). These initiatives begin to provide a structure of support for students that results in improving the climate. State initiatives fall into several categories: addressing minority concerns in all statewide plans and the development of special plans for diverse students; better coordination and collaboration between K–12 education and higher education to find solutions to educational problems; finance strategies that include performance funding, competitive grant programs, and need-based financial aid; and policies that "view assessment as a way to measure institutional effectiveness in meeting the educational needs of students" (Matthews 1996, p. 108). Six common strategies in various states include outreach programs for schools, recruitment and retention programs for graduate and professional schools, the development of comprehensive academic services, precollege preparatory efforts, need-based financial aid, and development programs for faculty and administrators (Callan 1988). Two less common but also important strategies include mechanisms for monitoring the achievement of minority groups and articulation programs for transfer students to improve movement from community colleges, which large numbers of students of color attend, to four-year institutions.

"Creating a sound state-level strategy for eliminating educational disparities requires sustained commitment, adequate resources, and a willingness to take risks and experiment" (Callan 1994, p. 337). Given that equity and diversity are not always the top priority for colleges and universities, one of the most important roles of state elected and appointed officials is to ensure that these issues, so critical to society, are at the top of the list of higher education priorities in their state. Hence, the first priority of states "is to set the agenda, an agenda for sustained progress in the enrollment and achievement of underrepresented minorities" (p. 338). The goals should be extremely clear so that each institution's and state's degree of progress can be evaluated regularly. Finally, none of the policy recommendations that have been offered are more important or significant than the need for colleges and universities to reaffirm

> . . . the centrality of the teaching mission of colleges and universities, and the preservation of diversity of institutional mission within state higher education systems. All of the special programs, accountability, and other policies directed at minority student achievement in higher education will come to naught if they are put into place in policy and institutional environments where teaching and learning are denigrated (Callan 1994, p. 344).

In summary, state policy as evolved plays a significant role in improving the climate for diversity through directives, recommendations, and support for initiatives. Essentially, analysts have identified the need to fundamentally change institutions to ensure that the core teaching and learning activities are effective and inclusive.

Financial Aid and Maintaining Diversity in Students
Most state reports related to the goals of improving access and achievement for students repeatedly refer to the need to make adequate funding available to students to achieve those goals. Without a doubt, state and federal financial aid policies have facilitated the development of more diverse student bodies on college campuses. In reviews of the re-

search on the impact of student financial aid, researchers have found that financial aid generally does what it was created to do—increase access to higher education (St. John 1991a; Stampen and Fenske 1988). Financial aid increases the probability that students will attend college. But although all forms of aid have been found to be positively associated with the decision to attend college when *all* students are considered, not all forms of aid have been found to be equally effective in promoting access for students from historically disadvantaged backgrounds. Aid packages with loans have been found to be less consistently significant in facilitating access for minority applicants than they are for white applicants (St. John 1991a). How students and their families view loans may differ, as black, Latino, and American Indian students tend to borrow considerably less than white or Asian Pacific–Americans (Stampen 1985).

Many students from low-income families regularly experience other barriers to financial aid (Olivas 1986; Orfield 1992). Students and their families are frequently unaware of the programs available to them or what they must do to apply for aid. This lack of knowledge excludes students from receiving any aid or severely limits their choice of college. Further, once students and their families are aware of what types of financial aid may be available, they must find ways to successfully navigate a series of complex and comprehensive application forms. And although students and families from higher-income backgrounds are generally able to provide the information required as a matter of course, the process can be extremely difficult for students from lower-income backgrounds. Further exacerbating these problems is the fact that insufficient research has been conducted that can be helpful to policy makers as they consider the effect of the decisions they make about federal aid policies. Most of what we know about the impact of financial aid comes from students who are already in the higher education system. Not enough research has been done on those who are excluded or those who drop out before they can ever become part of the higher education system. Hence, we do not know enough about the impact of different types of financial aid on the decision-making processes of students who elect not to attend college.

Research that has been conducted, however, suggests that declines in federal grant programs between 1976 and 1984 had a detrimental effect on minority students' participation in higher education (St. John 1991a, 1991b). A study of the high school class of 1982 found that the enrollment decisions of low-income students are price-responsive to grants but not to loans, while middle-income students are more price-responsive to loans than to grants (St. John 1990). Several researchers suggest that increases in federal student grant funding would be the most efficacious way to promote minorities' access in the short run and is an essential element of any long-term strategies devised to increase access and persistence (Astin 1982; St. John 1991b). The increased funding of loans combined with the availability of loan funds for middle-income students helps us to understand why total enrollments remained higher than had been projected during the 1980s despite declines in minority participation rates (St. John 1991a). In this case, changes to financial aid programs appear to have conflicting outcomes with regard to the goal of increased access to higher education. The expanded availability of and extended eligibility for loan dollars (and the decreased availability of grant and work study funds) have promoted access for students from middle-income families while restricting the access of students from low-income backgrounds. Based on a review of research assessing the impact of student financial aid, St. John (1991a) asserts that large levels of debt are likely to have a negative influence on persistence to degree completion.

The prevailing political climate is characterized by politicians who are enamored of crackdowns on loan defaulters, the elimination of scholarships for minorities, and relief for the middle class (Orfield 1992). Although the effect of these decisions has been felt in the 1980s and 1990s, the seeds for these changes to the financial aid system were sewn during the 1970s "when a politically irresistible but extremely expensive idea came into federal policy: the idea of extending aid to the middle class" (p. 345). After controlling for inflation, federal funds fell by 5 percent during this time, while tuition and fees rose by 40 percent (Orfield 1992). These changes required more students to find work, "a process that was particularly damaging to poorly prepared low-income students" (p. 359). Moreover, during this time opportunities for work study (which has been shown to be more efficacious in facilitating the academic success of low-income students and students of color) declined as distribution of these funds moved in favor of students from higher-income backgrounds (Orfield 1992). The assumption made by policy makers that students and their families are the major source of college funding is unrealistic for low-income students. By way of illustration, consider that low-income students attending public or private colleges who receive the maximum federal and state assistance as well as provide the amount that the family can afford to contribute "still fall short of meeting the full cost of college. In public colleges the average aid package fell 15 percent short, and in private schools it was 30 percent short" (p. 360).

Although the decline in access and equality of opportunity for students from low-income backgrounds that results from decreased funding of financial aid programs should be sufficient rationale for policy makers to reconsider the negative effect these changes have had over the past two decades, the funding of federal aid programs is threatened each budget year. Decreased funding of federal aid programs makes even less sense when we consider financial aid as a form of investment of public funds. One helpful way to think of financial aid in this way is to calculate the return on investment of public funds in federal aid that accrues from the tax revenue they generate. Based on data from the National Longitudinal Study of the High School Class of 1972 and data from the Current Population Surveys of 1979 and 1980, "the net present value of each dollar invested in student aid during the 1970s was about $4.30" (St. John and Masten 1990, p. 19). In other words, every dollar invested in federal aid programs during the 1970s created an additional $4.30 in tax revenues that otherwise would not have been collected. Based on the results of their analyses, the authors argue that investing in student financial aid may be the most profitable investment the federal government can make with its funds.

To summarize, the funding of federal aid programs for students has not kept pace with increases in tuition. The findings of research on the impact of financial aid indicate that recent federal policies related to financial aid continue to present barriers for poor families from various racial and ethnic groups, detrimentally affecting equity and access to college (Orfield 1992). A key component of any long-term or short-term response to these trends should involve substantial increases in federal funding for student grants rather than an increased emphasis on loans (St. John 1991b). Finally, research indicates that the funding of federal financial aid programs provides a substantial return on investment of public funds (St. John and Masten 1990). Maintaining good state and federal financial aid programs is critical to maintaining the diversity of student enrollments that institutions have achieved in the last few decades.

From Research to Practice

Research over recent years has brought focus to various dimensions of the campus climate for diversity so that we better understand institutions and their impact on students, students' responses to the climate on campus, and relationships that develop among diverse students and faculty. Although many institutions still contend with issues of diversifying their student body, more campuses need information that will move them beyond these issues to address the psychological and behavioral dimensions of the climate. More individuals from institutions are talking about improving the climate at national higher education conferences and are engaged in sharing practices that work. The empirical evidence provided here can enable institutional administrators and program planners to benefit from a wealth of research that has been focused on specific institutions as well as research that spans a broad national representation of students and institutions. Many institutions are assessing their climate for diversity to better understand their own institutional contexts. A wealth of knowledge is now available, and institutions are better informed so they can begin to examine their campus culture. Designing an action plan that will significantly improve the quality of the experience for undergraduates is perhaps the next important challenge in the process. The next section enumerates some general principles for improving the climate for diversity that are derived from the empirical research studies and state policy reports reviewed thus far. These principles can serve as the basis for institutional practice and program development.

DESIGN PRINCIPLES FOR IMPROVING THE CLIMATE FOR DIVERSITY IN HIGHER EDUCATION INSTITUTIONS

The increased cultural diversity of the nation's campuses challenges institutions of higher education to achieve fundamental change. Over the past 50 years, campuses in this country have enrolled students and hired faculty and staff who represent a broader variety of races, ethnicities, and cultures than at any previous time in history. Among the forces fueling these dramatic changes have been armed international conflict, changes in the world economic order, major social movements, presidential Executive Orders, government legislation, federal court rulings, and increased immigration. In the process, the country has been required to confront the myth of America as a homogeneous nation in the stark light cast by a reality that is decidedly multiracial, multicultural, and heterogeneous.

Universities and colleges that imagined themselves to be, and functioned as, Eurocentric institutions are now required to "reinvent" themselves. The challenge is a daunting one, the question how an institution changes. Evidence of failed attempts at improving the campus climate for diversity is readily provided by reports of palpable racial tension, periodic racial conflict, student protests, and persistent racial inequality in terms of representation on the nation's campuses. Some answers, however, are provided by our review of empirical research literature. The review reveals key, consistent findings that point toward strategies for improving the campus climate for diversity in U.S. higher education. Moreover, the research reveals how various dimensions of diversity, particularly contact with diverse peers, are related to a wide range of learning and democratic outcomes that will prepare students for making decisions, living, and working in a diverse society.

In articulating design principles for improving the campus climate for diversity, we begin first by acknowledging the complex system of relationships involved. Campuses are complex social systems defined by the relationships maintained between people, bureaucratic procedures, structural arrangements, institutional goals and values, traditions, and the larger sociohistorical environments where they are located. Therefore, any effort to redesign campuses with the goal of improving the climate for racial and cultural diversity must adopt a comprehensive approach. Moreover, it must be understood that the goal of achieving positive change in these institutions will require a long-term perspective. Institutions are slow to change: It is the nature of a stable system of higher education.

Thus, the success of efforts to achieve institutional change will rely on leadership, firm commitment, adequate resources, collaboration, monitoring, and long-range planning.

Institutional change can be implemented at several levels; foremost is the structural or concrete level. Observable evidence of cultural diversity must be present on campus. One should see increases at all levels of the institution (i.e., students, faculty, staff, administrators) in the number of previously excluded and underrepresented racial/ethnic minorities. Ideally, minorities should be represented on the campus in proportionate numbers. Although efforts to increase the representation of minorities on campus and to remove barriers to their participation are crucial, these steps alone are not sufficient to achieve the goal of improving the climate for diversity.

Beyond the physical, observable characteristics of a campus are the attitudinal and behavioral characteristics that shape the institution's climate. These dimensions of the institutional climate are an important consideration, because they best characterize how particular groups of individuals on campus "feel" and relate with each other. In this respect, it is necessary to examine how the campus feels from the perspective of minority individuals (Do they feel welcome? Do they sense hostility? Do they feel valued?) and how the campus responds to the presence of racially and culturally different groups (Does the campus strive to change to incorporate these students, or does the campus feel that only the minority students need to change? Does the campus genuinely value diversity?). In short, two sets of issues emerge: (1) How diverse does the campus look in the representation of different cultural groups, and (2) to what extent does the campus operate or function like a multicultural institution?

The following design principles outline strategies to achieve an improved campus climate for diversity. The principles are stated as general concepts or guiding precepts that emerged from the review of empirical studies and state policy documents. They include specific strategies focused on the critical actors that play a role in determining the campus climate for diversity (administrators, faculty, staff, and students).

1. *Affirm the goal of achieving a campus climate that supports racial and cultural diversity as an institutional priority.* To have real credence, the goal of an improved campus climate for diversity must be affirmed as an

institutional priority, requiring that administrators, staff, faculty, and students in leadership positions identify it as an important goal. Beyond stating that diversity is important, these campus leaders must be able to understand and articulate how diversity serves the larger goals of the academy. In times of increased racial inequality and division in racial attitudes in the general society, higher education institutions play a key role in the education of our future leaders, who will live in an increasingly multicultural society. Campus leadership will also need to recognize and to advocate the inseparable tie between diversity and academic excellence without diminishing one or the other. Unless the goal of creating a diverse learning environment is viewed as an integral component and necessary to achieve academic excellence, the goal will be considered separate or antithetical, thus inclining the campus community to devalue diversity.

2. *Systematically assess the institutional climate for diversity in terms of historical legacy, structural diversity, psychological climate, and behavioral elements to understand the dimensions of the problem.* Central to the process of improving the climate for diversity on college campuses is a recognition and an understanding of the dimensions of the problem. Actors and programs at the institution must engage in a deliberate, self-conscious process of self-appraisal. Such assessments will provide baseline information on the current state of affairs regarding the campus climate for diversity. In most instances, this process of self-study will be formal, perhaps requiring the creation of commissions or committees whose charge is to examine the structural diversity, psychological climate, and behavioral patterns in campus departments, procedures, and informal social settings. In addition, recent challenges to affirmative action practices that focus on structural diversity may require that campuses actually document the historical legacy of exclusion of various groups as well as the continuous barriers faced by specific groups in admissions, hiring, and retention. In addition to gathering data on the climate from institutional records and survey instruments, the campus community should also be encouraged to en-

gage in less formal activities, such as group discussions and the examination of prevailing attitudes of individuals on campus. The end goal of these formal and informal self-appraisal activities will be to systematically educate the campus and devise policies that address the factors that facilitate or block efforts to achieve an improved campus climate for diversity.

3. *Guided by research, experiences at peer institutions, and results from the systematic assessment of the campus climate for diversity, develop a plan for implementing constructive change that includes specific goals, timetables, and pragmatic activities.* This place is where most efforts to achieve institutional change flounder. As a rule, academics excel at researching and describing problems. We tend to be weak, however, when it comes to developing practical plans that systematically address identified problems. Another commonly encountered error takes the form of efforts to develop and execute plans without the benefit or guidance of empirical data. In this instance, plans that include specific goals, timetables, areas of responsibility, and practical activities, informed by empirical study of the problem, can be developed and implemented. Such plans would be developed for the campus as a whole and for each key academic department and service unit of the university. The campuswide plan would provide the template on which other plans for departments, classrooms, or service units would be based.

4. *Implement a detailed and ongoing evaluation program to monitor the effectiveness of and build support for programmatic activities aimed at improving the campus climate for diversity.* Changes in procedures or rules and newly instituted programs must be tracked to ensure that the desired effects are achieved. Data from such evaluations would also provide an excellent source of guidance for making required modifications. Evaluative data represent an excellent basis for making informed choices about how best to allocate scarce resources between competing programs. Moreover, such data provide a record that can inform efforts by peer institutions to improve the campus climate for diversity. Finally, the

periodic reports that flow from such evaluations can help to keep the campus engaged in and informed about the institution's efforts to change. Keeping the issue before the campus community creates a forum whereby success can be celebrated and shortcomings identified and corrected. Perhaps more important, successes in developing a supportive climate for diversity can engender public support for institutional initiatives and have the effect of attracting more students, faculty, and staff who wish to be affiliated with such a learning and work environment.

In general, these first four design principles incorporate key components: emphasizing campus climate as a priority, fact finding about the current status of the campus climate, designing and implementing a plan for constructive change, and monitoring the effectiveness of the plan for achieving change. Each component—setting priorities, fact finding, programming, and evaluating results—should be part of any effort to change the institutional climate at many levels (e.g., university, college, department, classroom, dormitory). The next principles are derived from key research findings that can be the basis for new programs and policies geared toward improving the campus climate.

5. *Create a conscious effort to rid the campus of its exclusionary past, and adopt proactive goals to achieve desegregation that includes increasing opportunity for previously excluded groups.* Most campuses have gone about the business of showing the public how much they have accomplished in diversifying their environments. But it is always more difficult to genuinely assess the many ways a history of exclusion has been perpetuated or how little has been accomplished in terms of creating a more inclusive environment. To support specific efforts, particularly in the area of campus affirmative action programs, campuses may need to acknowledge how much their exclusionary past continues to influence who attends or seeks employment at their institution. Thus, instead of ignoring their past, institutions should take it into account so they can assess how much has been accomplished and, more important, identify areas that continue to harbor the vestiges of exclusion. After an

honest assessment, the institution might draft statements affirming its commitment to inclusiveness and renouncing its exclusive past. The president can also disseminate statements in a series of high-profile speeches.

In seeking remedies for an exclusionary past, the goal for desegregation should be to increase educational opportunity for those who have been historically underrepresented, which translates into creating better environments for students to learn and develop on both predominantly white and predominantly black campuses. Increasing students' options for choice of college allows for greater overall educational opportunity and can be achieved by paying attention to improvements in programs and support systems at predominantly white institutions, and by enhancing the resources and academic programs on predominantly black campuses, tribal colleges, and Hispanic-serving institutions.

Faculty can serve as a positive normative group to improve the climate for diversity through their roles as teachers, producers of new knowledge, and participants in institutional governance.

6. *Involve faculty in efforts to increase diversity that are consistent with their roles as educators and researchers.* Research evidence shows that the normative environment as represented by the attitudes and values of faculty on different campuses affects the attitudes of students. Faculty can serve as a positive normative group to improve the climate for diversity through their roles as teachers, producers of new knowledge, and participants in institutional governance. At the same time, faculty may need assistance in dealing with the social conflicts, stereotypes, and misconceptions among diverse groups of students that are likely to manifest themselves in the classroom. Institutions can introduce programs that help faculty manage classroom conflict, create opportunities for open discussion of diversity, and become aware of their own attitudes and their effects on the students they teach. This approach goes beyond sensitivity training in that it provides faculty with the tools to manage classroom dynamics that create important learning experiences with diverse student groups.

7. *Create collaborative and cooperative learning environments where students' learning and interaction among diverse groups can be enhanced.* Faculty can adopt pedagogical practices that structure opportunities to pro-

mote relationships and interactions across racial and ethnic groups. These activities might include the development of topical study groups, group projects as part of the evaluation of students' work, or the creation of a community service component for classroom material. In short, faculty can increase students' interaction and provide students with the opportunity to learn more about each other, as well as more about the specific content areas in a course. Campuses can provide incentives and rewards to support the redesign of courses using more cooperative or collaborative models.

8. *Increase students' interaction with faculty outside class by incorporating students in research and teaching activities.* Research indicates that increased interaction between faculty and students typically results in more positive achievement for students. Students in one study were likely to report higher GPAs when they reported higher levels of out-of-class contact with faculty, were exposed to faculty who used nontraditional teaching styles, and had faculty who reported higher levels of satisfaction with their jobs. African-American students in particular, however, were much less likely to have high levels of out-of-class contact with faculty. The climate at the institution and students' achievement can be improved by ensuring that broad segments of students have opportunities to interact formally and informally with faculty. Many large research universities, for example, have created opportunities for undergraduates to participate with faculty in research projects.

9. *Initiate curricular and cocurricular activities that increase dialogue and build bridges across communities of difference.* Specific curricular and cocurricular activities can be implemented on college campuses to improve students' knowledge base, attitudes, and values, and increase understanding across communities of difference. Student peer groups have mixed effects on support for campus diversity; cliques or noninclusive peer groups are most likely to have negative effects on students' attitudes and acceptance of others from different backgrounds. At the same time, students need to maintain their own peer groups, because they provide social comfort and a sense

of affiliation, and enhance identity for individuals. Informal dialogue groups or sessions affiliated with formal academic coursework provide both a structure and a process for addressing the intergroup dynamics of multiculturalism in the learning environment. Student affairs professionals or faculty can train student peers to facilitate such dialogues and offer opportunities for involvement throughout the academic year.

College programming can also include a series of multicultural programs that celebrate the history and cultures of different racial/ethnic students and provide incentives for students from other backgrounds to participate. Campuses need to provide support for strong ethnic identities and affiliations as well as provide institutional encouragement for multiracial contacts.

10. *Create a student-centered orientation among faculty and staff.* Student-centered campuses, or those that emphasize students' academic and personal development, more often exhibit low tension among diverse groups. Campuses that contain essential elements of a student-centered orientation create validating experiences for students from different backgrounds and a welcoming environment that enhances the climate for diversity and development. Faculty and administrators can convey an interest in students' academic and personal development and create an environment where students feel valued, thereby significantly reducing feelings of competition among groups on campus. Developing a student-centered orientation in the classroom suggests significant changes in understanding how much students learn and how approaches to teaching must be modified. In short, a student-centered orientation is reflected by the institution's priorities as well as by the activities of the college's personnel.

11. *Include diverse students in activities to increase students' involvement in campus life. Ensure that programming for diversity involves general support services as well as coordinated activities and support programs for students of color.* Campus climates that encourage students' involvement more often support diversity. Participation in racially focused activities and support programs (for

example, the Black Student Union and minority peer support services) is associated with African-Americans' higher social involvement, informal social interactions with faculty, and higher use of general support services. Such programs and activities function as part of a larger safety net, encouraging students to take advantage of many other services and activities offered. In the absence of such programs, it is not clear whether students would take advantage of some mainstream services or have opportunities for leadership in typical college activities. Thus, campuses would do well to develop a wide range of coordinated support services to meet students' needs.

12. *Increase sensitivity and training of staff who are likely to work with diverse student populations.* Administrators can shape the climate for diversity on campus and may unknowingly thwart students' success. Administrators have been cited as a source of discrimination that was a key contributor to a diminished sense of belonging among students attending predominantly white institutions. These findings call for increased cultural sensitivity training among administrators and underscore the importance of ensuring that all groups are treated fairly in campus policies. Hiring individuals with experience in multicultural settings and who have conflict management skills, or providing such training to existing staff will help to provide the kind of staff that can promote students' success.

These 12 research-based principles are intended to guide various levels of practice from the planning stages at a more central level of administration through implementation of specific initiatives that engage individual faculty and students. In addition, the principles take campuses in the direction of maximizing the benefits of the racial/ethnic diversity they have been able to achieve through recruitment. Implementation of the principles may reinvigorate existing programs or require the design of new initiatives where none have previously existed. The next section provides specific illustrations of how the principles could work in practice.

EXAMPLES OF PROMISING PRACTICE

The first part of this report presents a framework for conceptualizing the racial climate on campus. Within the context of the four dimensions of campus climate, the results of a synthesis of research indicate that the racial climate on campus reflects a dynamic relationship among these dimensions. Perhaps most important, each dimension is also related to specific learning and democratic outcomes for students. Based on our understanding of these research findings, the second part of this monograph suggests 12 principles that can guide those who are interested in creating and designing a positive climate for racial/ethnic diversity on campus. The third design principle recognizes that the experience and knowledge that other institutions have in designing and implementing diversity-related programs can be invaluable to institutions that wish to engage in a similar process. The remainder of this report describes and discusses examples of what we believe to be "promising practice."

The highlighted programs first came to our attention from one of four sources: (1) information gathered in a national survey of campuses conducted by the American Council on Education (ACE); (2) information on diversity initiatives funded by the Ford Foundation; (3) information on diversity initiatives funded by the Fund for the Improvement of Post Secondary Education (FIPSE); and (4) information provided by colleagues who are actively involved in these programs. Because of the comprehensive nature of the information gathered by ACE, our search for examples of promising practice focused primarily on this information. The results of this survey were published in 1993 in *Sources: Diversity Initiatives in Higher Education.** The survey did not make any judgments as to the quality or success of the programs; rather, its primary goal was to compile and present relevant information about the various existing initiatives. ACE hoped that its efforts would "fill an information void and serve to expand the sup-

---

Sources is the first national publication that provides summary information on organizational, institutional, state, and federal programs specific to multicultural initiatives in higher education. Although by no means inclusive of all higher education initiatives that focus on people of color, the publication does provide a sizable sample of current efforts in the field. *Sources* includes entries for more than 1,200 regional and national organizations, colleges and universities, state, local, and federal agencies, and governing boards. Synoptic descriptions of more than 2,000 curriculum projects, discipline-related initiatives, faculty development programs, and efforts to recruit and retain students are included (American 1993, p. ix).

---

port network among campus administrators and faculty members who are seeking to effect long-term and systemic changes that will result in the education and employment of more people of color on college campuses" (American 1993, p. ix).

We worked in collaboration with an ACE staff member, who searched this database for key words and phrases related to programs and/or practices addressing race relations on campus. The search enabled us to identify about three dozen programs that we thought exemplified "promising practice" on campus. Although we were initially disheartened by the small number of programs we were able to highlight, we think it may be a result of our effort to highlight programs and practices that best exemplify the framework and design principles described earlier. Many very good and worthwhile programs are available, but many of them contain very few of the design principles deemed critical to improving the campus climate. We selected a few exemplars that indicate a strong bent toward improving the climate and making the most of the diverse learning environments achieved.

We also reviewed information on diversity-related programs funded by the Ford Foundation and FIPSE. In the case of the Ford Foundation, we selected programs whose descriptions fit one or more of the design principles. In the case of programs funded by FIPSE, we reviewed program descriptions for the 1990 through 1994 funding years that were designated "multicultural," "race relations," or "diversity." For the most part, these programs are focused on curriculum or directed at increasing the number of students of color in specific fields where these populations have traditionally been underrepresented.

We contacted institutional representatives and asked them to provide more detailed information about their programs and any evaluative data gathered. Based on the information provided, we initially identified what we thought were nine examples of promising practice. Within a short time, two of these programs no longer existed, indicating perhaps that even good programs are not viewed as central to an institution's objectives. The following pages provide seven descriptions of diversity-related initiatives that we believe exemplify promising practice as well as a sustained or long-term institutional commitment. The descriptions are based on the information program contact people provided us, and even though some of them may have changed from their initial models or contacts may have changed, they remain good practices that can be widely adopted. Some of these initiatives have been in place for nearly 10 years, indicating that both program contacts and aspects of the initiative have changed over time and presumably have grown with experience.

Although the descriptions are not exhaustive, we think they do provide a means for stimulating discussion regarding what a promising practice looks like. It is our hope that this information will stimulate educators to consider how they can act to improve the climate for racial/ethnic diversity on their campuses to enhance the learning environment.

Intergroup Relations Center: Arizona State University

In his inaugural speech at Arizona State University, President Lattie Coor identified cultural diversity as one of the four pillars of his plan for the growth and continued development of the university. Moreover, effort continues at the university to recruit and retain students, staff, and faculty from diverse backgrounds and experiences. Although this increased diversity provides the university with many opportunities, it also creates numerous challenges to be addressed. In May 1996, the provost appointed a task force of students, staff, and faculty and charged them with developing a plan for a center on the ASU campus that would address these challenges in terms of intergroup relations. In August 1997, the Intergroup Relations Center first opened.*

The primary mission of the Intergroup Relations Center (IRC) is to promote positive intergroup relations among students, staff, and faculty and to improve the campus climate for diversity at ASU. The IRC focuses on intergroup dynamics within the context of an institution of higher education and promotes change in intergroup relations at the personal, group, and structural levels. The process of change is participatory and collegial. The core assumption guiding the work and activities of the IRC is that diversity is an asset and can be used to enhance the growth of the ASU community in ways that achieve specific educational outcomes.

The IRC has adopted a set of guiding principles and practices that govern its operation through intergroup relations. Its

---

*Contact: Jesús G. Treviño, Director, Intergroup Relations Center, Arizona State University, A262 Student Services Building, Tempe, AZ 85287-1512, (602) 965-1574.

activities are undertaken in a manner that respects the dignity, worth, and security of all participants. All the center's activities are consistent with ethical procedures and guidelines set by the American Psychological Association and the university. Activities are designed to be bidirectional, multidimensional, inclusive, and interactive. Core concepts included in the training offered by the IRC include ingroup-outgroup dynamics, personal identity, social identity, social identity development, categorization, stereotyping, management of intergroup conflict and tension, and cross-cultural communication. Activities are designed to provide students, staff, and faculty with practical strategies and skills they can use when dealing with tension and conflict between groups. Finally, these activities occur with the expressed intent of decreasing intergroup conflict and discrimination on the ASU campus.

The IRC lists three primary goals that guide its activities. First, the center provides intergroup education and training to the campus community. As part of this goal, the IRC provides conflict prevention and mediation services for the campus. Second, the IRC serves as a clearinghouse for information about intergroup relations at ASU. This information includes intergroup training and education, discrimination, hate crimes, intergroup conflict on campus, and programs and initiatives on campus for reducing prejudice and discrimination. Third, the IRC provides support for research on the impact of programs and activities on intergroup relations as well as information that faculty can use to revise and develop curricula.

The IRC's current activities include Leadership 2000, Voices of Discovery (as intergroup dialogue program), Diversity in the Classroom: Prospects and Challenges, and a variety of workshops and training sessions prepared and presented by IRC staff for ASU students, staff, and faculty. Leadership 2000 trains students to positively and effectively address issues of diversity at ASU and in the greater society. The program promotes positive intergroup relations by creating awareness of the differences and commonalties that exist among people.

Voices of Discovery is a six-week cocurricular program that helps to promote greater understanding among different groups by bringing individuals from diverse groups together for honest, reflective, face-to-face dialogue in a safe context guided by trained facilitators. Participants in the program are typically also enrolled in university courses that address topics related to diversity, allowing participants to integrate theoretical understandings, learn such skills as active listening and conflict management, and gain a personal understanding of issues related to diversity. The program builds on a diversified curriculum and a diverse study body to create a link between students' cognitive and affective development, allowing students to apply the concepts they learn to their daily encounters with people from other communities.

Diversity in the Classroom is a four-week training program sponsored by the IRC and the English Department that examines the prospects and challenges of diversity in the classroom. The program's objective is to empower instructors to understand and use diversity in the classroom for achieving desired educational outcomes by focusing on social identity, free speech, constructive dialogue, and the deescalation of conflict.

Multimedia Packages on Dispute Resolution and Diversity: Carnegie Mellon University

Carnegie Mellon received support from FIPSE to develop and implement CD-ROM materials that teach college students how to resolve conflict and how to interact with others from diverse backgrounds. One goal of the CDs is to facilitate more widespread teaching of conflict resolution skills.*

Carnegie Mellon has developed two interactive multimedia packages to help students learn how to resolve disputes. *Allwyn Hall* enables college students to learn and practice basic conflict skills; *In All Respects* explores issues arising from cultural diversity on campus. The materials developed in this project can be used in a variety of settings, including courses and student life activities.

Allwyn Hall teaches a three-stage problem-solving process by presenting conflict scenarios for students to explore and resolve. Students work through the conflicts by listening and summarizing, clarifying the problems, and running brainstorming sessions. The CD-ROM is built around a simple navigable interface and videos of realistic conflicts that might arise in residence halls. The content of the program reflects recent experience, and research and theory in building conflict-management skills. The design incorporates findings about how multimedia can maximize acquisition and transfer of the necessary skills.

---

*Contact: Martha Harry or Preston Covey, Carnegie Mellon University, CAAE, Pittsburgh, PA 15213-3890, (412) 268-8532.

In All Respects includes a series of programs that explore racism, sexism, homophobia, and other issues affecting the campus climate. Students view videos and put together news stories about the issues. Their studies are then evaluated for representation and balance of diverse viewpoints. The first program, "An Editorial on Racism," exists in prototype and is currently being tested. A second program dealing with sexism is planned. Carnegie Mellon's project includes a plan describing a detailed program of evaluation.

In addition, UCLA administrators took an in-depth look at the demographics of the institution, in particular the racial breakdown, to assess what needs for diversity should be met.

Conflict Mediation Program: University Of California at Los Angeles

Today, about half of UCLA's undergraduates are students of color. Along with the University of California at Berkeley, UCLA is now among the most ethnically diverse research universities in the country. As the diversity of UCLA increased dramatically, the institution sought ways it could successfully adapt to and fully benefit from its diversity. A key event in this process was the 1987 Chancellor's Conference on Diversity that was held over two and one-half days and attended by some 150 faculty, students, and administrators. At the conference, Chancellor (Emeritus) Charles E. Young, reasserting his commitment to diversity, created the Council on Diversity as his primary advisory body on improving the campus climate for diverse populations. Comprising 25 faculty, students, and administrators, the council met monthly to create an agenda of short- and long-term plans to enhance the campus climate and intergroup relations.*

During his last 10 years as chancellor of UCLA, Young made diversity an institutional priority. The university involved faculty in diversity initiatives as part of their normal roles as researchers and educators. In addition, UCLA administrators took an in-depth look at the demographics of the institution, in particular the racial breakdown, to assess what needs for diversity should be met. The Conflict Mediation Program (CMP) is one response to these perceived needs. It is an effort by the campus to rid itself of its exclusionary past and to adopt proactive goals to achieve desegregation, including increasing higher education opportunities for previously excluded groups.

*Contact: Howard Gadlin, UCLA Conflict Mediation Program, 75 Haines Hall, Box 951589, Los Angeles, CA 90095-1589, (310) 825-7627.

A major component of the council's long-term goals was to establish an organized research unit with the working designation Center for the Study and Resolution of Interracial/Interethnic Conflict. The center's purpose is to support and disseminate faculty research directed toward the theoretical examination of issues and problem solving related to intergroup conflict. The findings and activities of CMP provide the foundation for the center's long-term research and action-oriented agenda. These efforts are being funded by the Hewlett Foundation.

CMP is based on the conviction that urban universities, particularly in the largest American cities where extraordinary racial and cultural diversity is increasingly the norm, must address issues of intergroup conflict aggressively and systematically. CMP employs proven principles of conciliation, negotiation, and mediation, and serves as a laboratory for the development of new techniques for addressing conflict in diverse academic settings. Through a series of carefully planned academic activities around controversial issues, CMP provides occasions in which diversity-related tension and conflict can be examined without exacerbating preexisting or potential hostilities. CMP provides an institutional mechanism for identifying and evaluating potentially divisive attitudes and values, for drawing on relevant scholarly work related to racial and ethnic conflict, and for reducing some of the tensions that undermine the achievement of a broadly supportive campus environment. Thus, CMP helps to create a collaborative and cooperative learning environment where student learning and interaction can be enhanced.

The center's purpose is to support and disseminate faculty research directed toward the theoretical examination of issues and problem solving related to intergroup conflict.

CMP trains a cohort of approximately 45 UCLA students, staff, and faculty each year to design and implement activities aimed at mitigating diversity-related conflict. A fundamental premise of CMP is that racial tensions and similar hostilities intensify when no safe and legitimate means are available to express and resolve the underlying conflicts that feed them. Workshops are designed to help CMP participants develop the skills—negotiation and mediation techniques, cross-cultural communication, awareness of diverse cultures, facilitation of group discussion, design of proactive programs to resolve disputes—necessary to intervene in diversity-related disputes.

In addition, student members of the team enroll in a course called Diversity, Conflict, and Conflict Resolution offered by the Department of Education. The course examines principles of conflict and conflict resolution with an emphasis on the resolution of racial, ethnic, and other diversity-related conflicts. Two courses were added in fall 1997—a seminar titled Dynamics of Diversity taught by a professor of anthropology and an intensive writing workshop that is coordinated with the anthropology course. As part of the course, students are placed in internships in campus programs and agencies where they observe, study, and write about the dynamics of cross-group interactions and conflict.

Once trained, CMP members are available to work with conflicts associated with diversity as mediators or discussion facilitators. CMP members also conduct workshops throughout the campus, and initiate and lead a series of public discussions on provocative topical issues. Members are engaged in at least four forums per year. Undergraduate students who are CMP members receive a stipend of $1,000 for their participation each year. Participants trained through the program are expected to remain with their CMP team for at least one year.

The developers of the proposal for CMP identified one major stumbling block. They were concerned that diversity initiatives frequently do not reach the desired audience, and they often have a limited impact on those who are already sensitive to such issues. For these reasons, organizers feel that it is imperative that the program be better integrated into the university's structure.

Detailed and ongoing evaluation has been included in this project to monitor the effectiveness of and build support for programmatic activities aimed at improving the campus climate for diversity at UCLA.

Intergroup Dialogues: University of Michigan
The program on Intergroup Relations, Conflict, and Community (IGRCC) was created in 1988 at the University of Michigan during a time when racial and ethnic tensions, and social protest and student activism were prominent. The program's goals were to advance students' understanding of deeply rooted intergroup conflicts and to increase their skills in addressing issues related to conflict and community. The program "gives students both the academic background and social experience necessary for informed participation in a diverse democracy" (Schoem 1997, p. 139). It is offered as a partnership by the College of Literature, Science, and the Arts,

the office of the Vice President for Student Affairs, and the office of the Vice Provost for Academic and Multicultural Affairs. The program currently offers four major learning activities: (1) academic courses and first-year seminars; (2) intergroup dialogues; (3) student leadership development and staff training; and (4) workshops for student organizations.*

Academic courses are offered by faculty members from American culture, psychology, sociology, and women's studies. The classes offered through IGRCC include first-year seminars, sophomore and upper-division courses, community service learning courses, and minicourses (Schoem 1997). The IGRCC classes provide students with disciplinary and interdisciplinary perspectives on intergroup relations, conflict, and community.

The intergroup dialogues are a way to advance students' understanding of deeply rooted intergroup conflicts and to increase their skills in addressing conflict and community (Zúñiga and Nagda 1992). The dialogues usually occur between members of two self-identified social groups. The most common focus of intergroup dialogues is interracial/interethnic; examples of the types of dialogues that have been conducted include African Americans and Caucasians, people of color and Caucasians, African Americans and Jews, African Americans and Latinos, and African Americans and Asian Pacific–Americans. Dialogues can also be structured around gender or sexual orientation (for example, African-American men and African-American women, Asian-American men and Asian-American women, gay men and gay men, lesbians, bisexuals, and heterosexuals). Another set of dialogues focuses on religion (e.g., Christians and Jews). The dialogues provide a structure within the academy for students from different backgrounds and cultural identities to discuss commonalities, learn about differences, and address issues of conflict. Opening up the lines of communication can help to alleviate future misunderstandings based on race, enabling students to build bridges across communities of difference at the institution.

Training for the IGRCC program is designed to provide students with the skills they need to serve as facilitators of the intergroup dialogues. The program also provides training for

*Contact: Charles Behling or Teresa Brett, 1521 Alice Lloyd Hall, 100 Observatory, Ann Arbor MI 48109-2025, (313) 936-1875.

student staff who work in different student affairs offices across the campus. The goal is to harness the learning that occurs primarily through peers by training peers to facilitate the dialogues. The final aspect of the IGRCC program involves a variety of workshops that the IGRCC staff provide to different student groups, residence halls, and organizations on campus. These workshops generally address issues of intergroup relations and/or community-building activities on campus.

Diversity Opportunity Tool: Vanderbilt University

Most campuses across the country have faculty, students, and staff who are responsive to the call to embrace racial and ethnic diversity. Although they are willing to do something when they encounter malicious or unknowing acts of racial and ethnic insensitivity or intolerance, they may discount particular incidents as unintentional or insignificant, or may not know what to do that would make a difference. This lack of knowledge and personal confidence undermines their ability to change their own behavior or to try to educate others in ways that will help them change their behavior.

With funding from the university and from FIPSE, Vanderbilt developed the Diversity Opportunity Tool (DOT). DOT is a computer-based, interactive videodisc designed to deal with two major sources of tension and conflict among persons of different racial and ethnic groups: (1) inappropriate behaviors that derive from ignorance and ineptitude; and (2) behaviors that are racist in origin and are manifest because it is not clear what behaviors the culture of the institution will sanction. DOT can be used in two primary ways as part of an overall campus strategy to address racial discrimination. It can be used to change the behavior of individuals, and it can be used to manifest institutional norms of acceptance of racial and ethnic differences among members of the campus community.*

DOT is research based. That is, each response to the vignettes is supported with research information about the incident and the options for response. Hence, DOT links research to real-life challenges and uses data to support the arguments presented, allowing users to increase their knowl-

---

*Contact: Alma Clayton-Pedersen, Department of Leadership and Organizations, Vanderbilt University, Box 514 Peabody College, Nashville, TN 37203-5701, (615) 322-8000.

edge so that they can address and respond to situations of racial intolerance. In short, DOT assumes that certain members of the campus community will address racially motivated acts of intolerance and discrimination if they know how—and DOT tries to teach them how.

DOT simulates several common "critical incidents" of intolerance. Users' selection of an incident triggers a brief video depicting a typical incident of intolerance. Users are asked to select a response to the incident from a number of alternatives. The choice of a response triggers a vignette of the likely outcome of that response. The computer prompts users to seek further information and resources that would help in dealing with incidents of the kind being considered.

The goals were to develop a product that would identify incidents of intolerance and discrimination that are fairly common and generic in nature, use issues that have fairly clear solutions, provide sufficient useful information to fill change agents' and perpetrators' gaps in knowledge, provide resources for more in-depth discussion, provide a feasible means to challenge these common acts, develop a set of rules to guide change agents' productive behavior, and clearly articulate the goal of changing the campus environment to allow all members of a campus community to flourish.

Application of this technology has taken several forms, including use by individual students. DOT has been used as part of training for resident advisers of freshmen students at Vanderbilt. Over the same period, DOT has been shown to the entering freshman class as part of a series on freshman residential living. The most common use of DOT has been in conjunction with courses such as Small Group Behavior and Multicultural Issues. DOT can also be used in training graduate teaching assistants and new professors. Faculty may be more likely to use DOT, because it can be used privately, it is research-based, and it can be used as a teaching tool in many courses.

A facilitator's manual is available to help maximize the learning opportunities the tool can provide. A final report on DOT's development (which includes a description of the undergraduate course in which the concepts for the vignettes were developed and its evaluation) is available. DOT is currently being used at more than 40 campuses across the country and is still available for use by interested campuses.

Diversity Discussion Workbook: A Collaboration

A collaborative effort of the Ohio State University, University of North Carolina, and University of Washington Schools of Law helped to produce the Diversity Discussion Workbook. The workbook consists of vignettes, sample scripts, creative writing to explore diversity, tips for discussion leaders, and a complete bibliography. Each component is an integral part of the schools' efforts to improve the climate for diversity on campus.*

The vignettes display the different places where diverse student groups come into contact with each other, from the snack bar to the classroom. For example, four white students are clustered at one of three tables in the law school snack bar, while two African-American students sit at another table. Two more African-American students enter the room and pause as they decide where to sit. One student grabs the other and pulls him toward the African-American table. The vignette is followed by discussion questions, one of which asks, "What is going on here?"

This format is designed to promote open discussion among faculty, staff, and students. The discussion questions are designed to initiate cocurricular and curricular activities that increase dialogue and build bridges across communities of difference. The sample scripts provide word-for-word transcriptions of the diverse interaction among students, staff, and faculty. The scripts encourage dialogue by making abstract situations more concrete. Moreover, each script is followed by additional discussion questions.

The third component of the Diversity Discussion Workbook uses creative writing to explore issues of diversity. By incorporating colorful language within the script format, the finished product more adequately reflects real life. In one scenario, for example, an African-American student asks an Asian student out on a date. Another Asian student overhears the interaction and purposely bumps into the African-American student. A heated exchange ensues. The writers of the scenario are able to capture the moment's intensity through the written word. This use of candid language encourages those who read the vignette to express themselves more honestly. It also encourages discussion and dialogue.

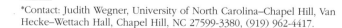

*Contact: Judith Wegner, University of North Carolina–Chapel Hill, Van Hecke–Wettach Hall, Chapel Hill, NC 27599-3380, (919) 962-4417.

The workbook provides tips for discussion leaders. The creators of the workbook encourage college administrators, faculty, and staff to use this tool with small groups of six to 10 students. Other directions contained in the workbook include information on spatial arrangements, communication, and styles of leadership for facilitators to use when working with the group. The bibliography lists the sources of the theory that serves as the underpinnings of the workbook.

A Design for Diversity: University of Wisconsin System
In 1988, the University of Wisconsin board of regents approved a 10-year systemwide plan to increase the presence of American Indian, African-American, Asian-American, and Latino/Hispanic students, faculty, and staff, and economically disadvantaged students in the University of Wisconsin system. The resulting Design for Diversity is aimed at creating a multicultural teaching and learning environment, one that effectively prepares all students to live and work in a pluralistic society. The plan targets institutional racism and seeks to eradicate its negative impact on the system's campuses.*

The plan lists seven goals:

1. Recognize the need to eliminate the underrepresentation of minority and economically disadvantaged people in the UW system.
2. Educate all students for an increasingly multicultural society in Wisconsin, the nation, and the world.
3. Improve recruiting and retention processes to enable targeted minority students to enroll more easily and function more effectively at the system's universities.
4. Improve evaluation efforts in the areas of minority student enrollment/retention and faculty/staff recruitment and retention.
5. Remove financial barriers that prevent minorities and economically disadvantaged people from viewing college as a realistic option.
6. Increase the number of minority faculty and staff throughout the UW system.
7. Establish effective partnerships with the public schools, state government, the community, and the private sector

---

*Contact: Hazel Symonette, University of Wisconsin System, Madison, WI 53715, (608) 262-2275.

to assist the UW system's efforts to improve minority education.

The Design for Diversity proposed a 100 percent increase in the number of new African-American, Latino/Hispanic, and American Indian freshman, transfer, and special undergraduate students between 1988 and 1998—from 1,270 to 2,540. Between 1988 and 1993, UW attained at least 80 percent of its goals for student enrollment each year. The system strives to retain the students recruited and to increase the number of underrepresented graduate students on its campuses.

The UW system actively seeks to enhance public discourse about cultural and socioeconomic diversity. The system's campuses offer a wide variety of speakers, workshops, symposia, conferences, exchange programs, publications, and academic courses exploring multicultural issues and concerns in addition to multicultural entertainment activities. They have implemented a requirement for organized courses or programs of instruction in ethnic studies as part of every student's undergraduate educational experience for either general education or graduation. Such efforts increase the potential for students' involvement in campus life. This programming to address diversity involves general support services for all students as well as support services directed primarily at students of color.

The UW system cites precollege programs as a strength in its efforts to recruit and retain underrepresented students. It has developed the UW Precollege Database, which distributes information about potential recruitment prospects to each UW campus. It is also committed to ensuring that appropriate support programs are in place before admitting students who are talented and motivated but may lack some academic prerequisites.

Further, the system seeks to remove financial barriers for minorities and disadvantaged people. Currently, the UW system has three financial aid programs for undergraduates targeting historically underrepresented racial/ethnic groups and two financial aid programs for graduate students. Based on what we know from our review of the literature regarding the impact of changes in financial aid, the UW system's efforts to increase the enrollment, retention, and graduation of underrepresented students depend greatly on its ability to provide appropriate amounts and types of aid for students.

The UW system continues to strengthen and streamline the collection, evaluation, and dissemination of information about enrollment and retention of minority students, and recruitment and retention of faculty and staff. In collaboration with the chancellor of each campus, the UW system president annually reviews the data to assess progress toward the goals of Design for Diversity.

Design for Diversity has set specific goals for hiring new faculty and staff from underrepresented populations. Exit interviews with departing faculty and staff of color provide each campus information about the reasons faculty and staff decide to leave campus. Evaluation also provides for review of all decisions not resulting in tenure or promotion of underrepresented faculty and staff.

Design for Diversity is making a conscious effort to rid the UW system of its exclusionary past, and to increase opportunity for previously excluded groups. The UW system seeks to establish partnerships with other educational and community-based organizations, and UW campuses have developed formal and informal partnerships with numerous tribal colleges, HBCUs, and Hispanic-serving institutions.

Moving from Principles to Practice

These promising practices, many of which began with chancellors and provosts who articulated the need for new initiatives to meet the needs of a diverse student body, reflect intentional ways that research-based design principles are enacted in diverse learning environments. The first design principle discusses the need for campuses to embrace diversity as a core institutional value. Of the examples of practice cited, the University of Wisconsin's Design for Diversity best illustrates this principle. In this plan, campus diversity is central to a 10-year plan for the statewide system of higher education.

The second design principle calls for systematic assessment of the campus climate for diversity within each of the four dimensions of our framework (historical legacy, structural diversity, psychological climate, and behavioral dimension). The fourth principle also calls for regular and ongoing assessment that monitors the effectiveness of efforts to increase diversity on campus. Although no immediate examples of assessment were this comprehensive, six of the seven programs highlighted earlier in this section are undertaking some form of assessment as part of the program. The

The first design principle discusses the need for campuses to embrace diversity as a core institutional value. Of the examples of practice cited, the University of Wisconsin's Design for Diversity best illustrates this principle.

success of these programs must be documented and begin to illuminate the ways in which they add value to the educational experience of students, preparing them to meet the demands of a complex, pluralistic society. Numerous studies have already been undertaken that provide information about not only the program's effectiveness but also how students learn in diverse environments. Individuals are encouraged to communicate with the contacts listed about the studies that are not yet published.

The third principle calls for the development of systematic plans for change that are informed by research, institutional assessment, and information from other similar institutions. Once again, the University of Wisconsin's Design for Diversity seems to best represent this principle. It is particularly effective in that it clearly articulates the desired outcomes and the time frame in which the goals are to be achieved.

The fifth principle addresses the need for campuses to recognize their history of exclusion and to engage in a process by which the campus rids itself of its exclusionary past. Our review of promising practices suggests that the Intergroup Relations Center at ASU, the Conflict Mediation Program at UCLA, and Design for Diversity of the UW system exemplify different ways in which institutions are accomplishing this goal.

The sixth principle calls for involving faculty in efforts to increase awareness of diverse cultures in ways that are consistent with their roles as educators and researchers. The IRC at Arizona State and the University of Michigan's program on Intergroup Relations, Conflict, and Community actively involve faculty in programs and activities. Both are linked with classes that often meet requirements for graduation and learning about the cultural legacies of our society. While the Voices of Discovery program at ASU is offered to augment activities conducted by faculty in the classroom, the IGRCC program at Michigan is now embedded in the curriculum and taught by faculty. Faculty also play an active role in training student peer facilitators who carry out class discussions and work in residence halls. UCLA also offers classes to students through its Center for the Study and Resolution of Interracial/Interethnic Conflict. Faculty involvement in development of the multimedia packages at Carnegie Mellon also seem to accomplish this objective. In each example, faculty gain expertise in managing diversity in the classroom, and learning how to turn conflict in the classroom into an opportunity to learn. Moreover, when faculty are involved in the evaluation of these programs, they bring their research expertise to these important questions of learning and intergroup dynamics.

The spirit of the seventh and ninth principles is perhaps best illustrated by dialogue groups at the University of Michigan, the Conflict Mediation Program at UCLA, and the Diversity Discussion Workbooks developed by the law schools at the Ohio State University, the University of North Carolina, and the University of Washington. These programs bring students together in ways that provide them with the tools and the motivation to talk about "differences." These activities are likely to empower students (as well as faculty and staff in the case of the IRC at ASU and the CMP at UCLA) in ways that will allow them to begin to build bridges across communities of difference.

The eleventh principle calls for activities that increase the involvement of diverse students in campus life. Some of these activities should be programs and support services that are directed primarily at students of color. In many ways, each program that we have discussed is consistent with this principle. They each consider the learning and improved relations that will allow students of color to interact on campus with confidence, understand the conflict that might surround them, and effectively feel a vital part of the activities that are central to the campus. When we add the eighth and tenth principles, we begin to get a better idea of ways our institutions might be transformed to make them more student-centered in their focus. It is clear from our review of the research that more student-centered colleges are likely to have a more supportive climate for racial/ethnic diversity on campus—benefiting *all* students on campus.

This discussion of evidence of the design principles in these examples of promising practice is not meant to be exhaustive. Clearly, evidence of many of the design principles can be found in each description. Rather, we present them as a guide for institutional leaders and educators who are interested in learning from the experience and success of others. With this information, we hope other institutions will be motivated to embrace intentional ways of improving learning environments.

CONCLUSIONS AND RECOMMENDATIONS

This report is titled "Enacting Diverse Learning Environments," because campuses have the capacity to improve a climate of common attitudes and perceptions. The climate for racial/ethnic diversity is subject to change, depending on the various dimensions presented in the conceptual framework: Campuses have been able to diminish racial incidents and campus protests, and improve intergroup relations by trying to overcome a historical legacy and image of exclusion, increasing structural diversity, creating structured learning opportunities for interaction across racial/ethnic communities, and attending to issues of diversity in the classroom through course content and pedagogy. Moreover, many have taken steps to create the conditions that maximize learning in diverse student environments, thereby preparing students for living and working in a society that is ever more complex and diverse. These activities are within the realm of campus planning, decision making, and coordination.

Because research on the climate reveals that it has the potential to affect students in many ways and that students' involvement with diverse peers results in greater educational benefits, it behooves institutions to more thoughtfully pursue intentional, sustained, and coordinated activities, recognizing students' natural need for affiliation with peers from the same background as a source of identity, familiarity, and comfort. At the same time, institutions should encourage students to engage with diverse peers, who may challenge their view of the world and expand their provincial vision. Otherwise, campuses can deepen social divisions that pervade a poor climate for diversity. Although many campuses have undertaken studies of campus climate, few institutions know what actions to take after they have examined the climate. Yet the research reveals that inaction or neglect of any one dimension of the climate will have undesirable consequences. It is important that campuses make a concerted effort to attend to the complexity of the diverse social environments they have created to realize the full learning potential of those environments.

Developing a Plan for Action

The research in this report provides compelling evidence for the difficulties inherent in and successful approaches to improving the climate for racial/ethnic diversity on a college campus. Gathering information about various dimensions of the climate unique to each campus can help identify areas of difficulty, but such activity should be followed by a plan of action. The conceptual framework and the design principles provided in this report are recommended as important starting points for campus-based discussion and evaluation. Several campuses have developed teams to discuss and address the climate for racial/ethnic diversity and used the framework to evaluate their array of current initiatives and plan new ones for the future. Campuses have held an event focused on improving the climate, bringing various constituencies to a "climate summit" to brainstorm ideas about future directions. Diversity is a characteristic of innovative organizations and can enhance creativity in small-group settings (Cox 1993). Therefore, the practices that ensure students' engagement with social difference and work to enhance learning in diverse environments also appear to work for the organization. The examples of practice cited in this report are evidence of initiatives that can be implemented systemwide at the organizational level by linking students' experiences inside and outside the classroom. Each example serves as a model of the many ways in which campuses proactively create the conditions that enhance learning in diverse environments.

Everyone Plays a Role in Improving the Climate
Over the years, college administrators have learned much about estimating the potential of students, and what they intuitively know about how to shape the diversity of an entering class turns out to have a powerful effect on the education of all students. Admissions officers play a key role in recruiting and admitting a student body that reflects a microcosm of the society we aspire to become. Although increasing the number of diverse students can change an image of a poor campus racial climate, efforts to sustain diversity in the learning environment can be hampered by a longstanding history of exclusion and reports of hostilities between groups. Admissions officers can offer information about the campus to focus individual recruits on other aspects of the college, but their "image management" also depends on the initiatives of other campus groups to improve the climate.

Similarly, student affairs professionals have intuitively worked with college peer groups and used peer education in a variety of student life programs. They are uniquely positioned to enhance learning for first-year students as they interact informally with diverse students from other backgrounds. In fact, student affairs professionals may have the best sense of the complexities inherent in creating a diverse learning environment, as their work is to serve diverse communities of students. A poor racial climate, however, stymies interaction across racially and ethnically diverse groups. Many in student affairs have engaged in efforts to maintain a climate of civility, attend to the specific needs of distinct racial/ethnic communities, and devise programs that build bridges across diverse communities. These latter initiatives must be extended to include intentional programs to enhance students' interaction across social differences outside the classroom as a way of enhancing educational outcomes that include cognitive growth, social development, and development as citizens of a diverse society. The work of student affairs professionals, then, is linked to faculty initiatives to promote learning in diverse environments.

College faculty play an important role in introducing the scientific knowledge and the multiple cultural legacies that make up a democratic and global society, including important values, skills, and knowledge that ensure graduates will be successful in diverse work environments. Their own values and approach to teaching influence students, as the research demonstrates, but they must also recognize that students might be learning a great deal more from their peers than they are from instructors in the classroom. This realization may be difficult to accept initially, but many faculty are beginning to recognize the potential of the college peer group and harness that influence to create more powerful learning environments in classrooms for all students. They play a key role in implementing all aspects of diversity in the classroom through the curriculum and through the pedagogy that engages students with each other and goes a long way toward improving the overall climate for diversity. The success of these initiatives, however, also depends on campus leaders who have a vision about what they would like to accomplish on campus.

Many campus administrators have organized strategic initiatives and plans to address racial/ethnic diversity on campus, but only a few have been explicit about the centrality of diversity to the campus's mission of improving teaching and learning. To their credit, campus administrative leaders have

To their credit, campus administrative leaders have articulated and reinforced diversity initiatives at every level of higher education ...

articulated and reinforced diversity initiatives at every level of higher education, provided the funds for initiatives, and coordinated activities that have resulted in marked changes in the institutional context for diversity. One of the greatest challenges for campus leaders is to organize efforts to develop a vision for the future. Several studies in this report suggest that diversity is linked in many ways with the central mission of teaching and learning. Therefore, such vision would incorporate diversity into the goals for the development of students' cognitive and affective skills that will be necessary for ethical decision making, commitment to the betterment of society, and negotiation of differences—inevitably part of a democratic society. The role of campus leaders in improving the climate is to develop a plan that integrates everyone as important parts of preparing students for the future, revitalizing a commitment to the education of students in a diverse learning environment.

Future Research as It Informs Practice
Although many researchers have measured the climate for racial/ethnic diversity from individual perspectives, the intent of this report is to highlight various interconnected dimensions of diversity on campus. In the real world, individual perceptions of the climate are informed by broader policy, a social historical context, and the specific history of the institution. Thus, no single element that informs individual perception should be analyzed alone. Continued research is recommended on these interrelationships and the complexities that diverse learning environments present to continue to help individuals understand the implications of their work on college campuses.

Further research is needed for understanding how structural diversity, the psychological climate, and interactions with diverse populations are all associated directly and indirectly with a broad range of educational outcomes. While the patterns across many studies identified in this report make a strong case for the educational value of diversity encountered in courses, programs, and informal interactions with peers, we recommend studies on new measures of educational outcomes that are linked with campus efforts to prepare students for a diverse democracy. This approach calls for new frameworks of diversity-related outcomes, more classroom-based studies to address how students learn in diverse environments, and additional research on integrated and coordinated efforts to enhance learning in diverse environments. Further, research on specific racial/ethnic groups helps inform our understanding of communities that experience the campus environment differently, and more research is needed on Asian Americans and Native Americans. In sum, across the range of studies reviewed, evidence suggests that higher education has learned much about educating a diverse student body in both research and practice. This report is an effort to highlight research that may move campuses toward addressing issues of campus climate and maximizing the learning that occurs in the diverse communities they have created.

REFERENCES

The Educational Resources Information Center (ERIC) Clearinghouse on Higher Education abstracts and indexes the current literature on higher education for inclusion in ERIC's database and announcement in ERIC's monthly bibliographic journal, *Resources in Education* (RIE). Most of these publications are available through the ERIC Document Reproduction Service (EDRS). For publications cited in this bibliography that are available from EDRS, ordering number and price code are included. Readers who wish to order a publication should write to the ERIC Document Reproduction Service, 7420 Fullerton Road, Suite 110, Springfield, Virginia 22153-2852. (Phone orders with VISA or MasterCard are taken at (800) 443-ERIC or (703) 440-1400.) When ordering, please specify the document (ED) number. Documents are available as noted in microfiche (MF) and paper copy (PC). If you have the price code ready when you call, EDRS can quote an exact price. The last page of the latest issue of *Resources in Education* also has the current cost, listed by code.

Abraham, A., and W. Jacobs. 1990. *Black and White Students' Perceptions of Their College Campuses.* Atlanta: Southern Regional Education Board. ED 326 094. 112 pp. MF–01; PC–05.

Adams, M., and Y. Zhou-McGovern. 1994. "The Sociomoral Development of Undergraduates in a 'Social Diversity' Course: Developmental Theory, Research, and Instructional Applications." Paper presented at an annual meeting of the American Educational Research Association, New Orleans, Louisiana. ED 380 345. 53 pp. MF–01; PC–03.

Allen, W.R. May/June 1987. "Black Colleges versus White Colleges: The Fork in the Road for Black Students." *Change:* 28–30.

———. 1988. "Black Students in U.S. Higher Education: Toward Improved Access, Adjustment, Achievement." *The Urban Review* 20: 165–67.

———. 1992. "The Color of Success: African-American College Student Outcomes at Predominantly White and Historically Black Public Colleges and Universities." *Harvard Educational Review* 62(1): 26–44.

Allen, W.R., E.G. Epps, and N.Z. Haniff, eds. 1991. *College in Black and White: African-American Students in Predominantly White and in Historically Black Public Universities.* Albany, N.Y.: SUNY Press.

Allen, W.R., and N. Haniff. 1991. "Race, Gender, and Academic Performance in U.S. Higher Education." In *College in Black and White: African-American Students in Predominantly White and in Historically Black Public Universities,* edited by W.R. Allen,

E.G. Epps, and N.Z. Haniff. Albany: SUNY Press.

Allport, G.W. 1954. *The Nature of Prejudice*. Reading, Mass.: Addison-Wesley.

Altbach, P.G., and K. Lomotey, eds. 1991. *The Racial Crisis in American Higher Education*. Albany, N.Y.: SUNY Press.

Alwin, D.F., R.L. Cohen, and T.M. Newcomb. 1991. *Political Attitudes over the Life Span: The Bennington Women after Fifty Years*. Madison: University of Wisconsin Press.

American Council on Education. 1993. *Sources: Diversity Initiatives in Higher Education*. Washington, D.C.: Author.

Antonio, A.L. 1998a. "The Impact of Friendship Groups in a Multicultural University." Doctoral dissertation, Univ. of California at Los Angeles.

——. 1998b. "Student Interaction across Race and Outcomes in College." Paper presented at an annual meeting of the American Educational Research Association, San Diego, California.

Asante, M.K., and H.S.N. Al-Deen. 1984. "Social Interaction of Black and White College Students: A Research Report." *Journal of Black Studies* 14(4): 507–16.

Asian Pacific American Education Advisory Committee. 1990. *Enriching California's Future: Asian Pacific Americans in the CSU*. Long Beach: California State Univ., Office of the Chancellor.

——. 1994. *Asian Pacific Americans in the California State University: A Follow-up Report*. Long Beach: California State Univ., Office of the Chancellor.

Association of American Colleges and Universities. 1985. *Integrity in the College Curriculum: A Report to the Academic Community*. Washington, D.C.: Author. ED 251 059. 62 pp. MF–01; PC not available EDRS.

——. 1995. *American Pluralism and the College Curriculum: Higher Education in a Diverse Democracy*. Washington, D.C.: Author. ED 398 783. 64 pp. MF–01; PC not available EDRS.

Astin, A.W. 1968. *The College Environment*. Washington, D.C.: American Council on Education.

——. 1982. *Minorities in American Higher Education*. San Francisco: Jossey-Bass.

——. 1985. *Achieving Educational Excellence*. San Francisco: Jossey-Bass.

——. 1988. "Student Involvement: A Developmental Theory for Higher Education." *Journal of College Student Personnel* 25(4): 297–308.

——. 1991. *Assessment for Excellence: The Philosophy and Practice of Assessment and Evaluation in Higher Education*. New

York: Macmillan.

————. 1993. *What Matters in College: Four Critical Years Revisited.*
San Francisco: Jossey-Bass.

Astin, A.W., H.S. Astin, A.E. Bayer, and A.S. Bisconti. 1975. *The*
Power of Protest. San Francisco: Jossey-Bass.

Astin, A.W., W.S. Korn, and E. Berz. 1991. *The American Freshman,*
1990. Los Angeles: Higher Education Research Institute. ED 351
908. 281 pp. MF–01; PC not available EDRS.

Astin, A.W., and R.J. Panos. 1971. "The Evaluation of Educational
Programs." In *Educational Measurement,* edited by R.L. Thorn-
dike. Washington, D.C.: American Council on Education.

Astin, A.W., J.G. Treviño, and T.L. Wingard. 1991. "The UCLA Cam-
pus Climate for Diversity: Findings from a Campuswide Survey
Conducted for the Chancellor's Council on Diversity." Los
Angeles: Higher Education Research Institute.

Bauer, K. 1998. *Understanding the Critical Components of Today's*
Colleges and Universities. New Directions for Institutional Research No. 98. San Francisco: Jossey-Bass.

Belenky, M., B. Clinchy, N. Goldberger, and J. Tarule. 1986. *Women's*
Ways of Knowing: The Development of Self, Voice, and Mind. New
York: Basic Books.

Bennett, C. 1984. "Interracial Contact Experience and Attrition
among Black Undergraduates at a Predominantly White University." *Theory and Research in Social Education* 12(2): 19–47.

Bennett, C., and A.M. Okinaka. 1990. "Factors Related to Persistence
among Asian, Black, Hispanic, and White Undergraduates at a
Predominantly White University: Comparisons between First- and
Fourth-Year Cohorts." *Urban Review* 22(1): 33–60.

Bernstein, A.R., and J.S. Eaton. 1994. "The Transfer Function: Build-
ing Curricular Roadways across and among Higher Education
Institutions." In *Minorities in Higher Education,* edited by M.J.
Justiz, R. Wilson, and L.G. Björk. Phoenix: ACE/Oryx.

Blake, E., Jr. 1991. "Is Higher Education Desegregation a Remedy
for Segregation but not Educational Inequality? A Study of the
Ayers v. Mabus Desegregation Case." *Journal of Negro Education*
60(4): 538–65.

Blalock, J.M. 1967. *Toward a Theory of Minority-Group Relations.*
New York: Wiley.

Bobo, L. 1983. "Whites' Opposition to Busing: Symbolic Racism or
Realistic Group Conflict?" *Journal of Personality and Social Psy-*
chology 45: 1196–1210.

Braddock, J.H. 1980. "The Perpetuation of Segregation across
Levels of Education: A Behavioral Assessment of the Contact

Hypothesis." *Sociology of Education* 53: 178–86.

———. 1985. "School Desegregation and Black Assimilation." *Journal of Social Issues* 41(3): 9–22.

Braddock, J.H., R.L. Crain, and J.M. McPartland. December 1984. "A Long-Term View of School Desegregation: Some Recent Studies of Graduates as Adults." *Phi Delta Kappan:* 259–64.

Braddock, J.H., and M. Dawkins. 1981. "Predicting Achievement in Higher Education." *Journal of Negro Education* 50: 319–27.

Braddock, J.H., and J.M. McPartland. 1982. "Assessing School Desegregation Effects: New Directions in Research." In *Research in Sociology of Education and Socialization.* Vol. 3. Greenwich, Conn.: JAI.

———. 1989. "Social-Psychological Processes That Perpetuate Racial Segregation: The Relationship between School and Employment Desegregation." *Journal of Black Studies* 19(3): 267–89.

Bunzel, J.H. 1992. "Race Relations on Campus: Stanford Students Speak." Stanford, Calif.: Stanford Alumni Association.

Cabrera, A.F., and A. Nora. 1994. "College Student Perceptions of Prejudice and Discrimination and Their Feelings of Alienation: A Construct Validation Approach." *Review of Education/Pedagogy/ Cultural Studies* 16(3–4): 387–409.

California Postsecondary Education Commission. 1990. *Toward an Understanding of Campus Climate: A Report to the Legislature in Response to Commission Report No. 90-19.* Sacramento: Author. ED 329 202. 74 pp. MF–01; PC–03.

Callan, P.M. 1988. "Minority Degree Achievement and the State Policy Environment." *Review of Higher Education* 11(4): 355–64.

———. 1994. "Equity in Higher Education: The State Role." In *Minorities in Higher Education,* edited by M.J. Justiz, R. Wilson, and L.G. Björk. Phoenix: ACE/Oryx.

Callan, P., and B. Finney. 1988. "State Policy and Minority Achievement in Higher Education." *Peabody Journal of Education* 66(1): 6–19.

Carter, D.F. 1997. "A Dream Deferred? Examining the Degree Aspirations of African-American and White College Students." Doctoral dissertation, Univ. of Michigan.

Carter, D.F., and R. Montelongo. 1998. "Being in the 'Minority': The Effect of Institutional Characteristics on the Degree Expectations of Students after Four Years." Paper presented at an annual meeting of the Association for the Study of Higher Education, Miami, Florida.

Carter, D.J., and R. Wilson. 1993. *Minorities in Higher Education: Eleventh Annual Status Report.* Washington, D.C: American

Council on Education. ED 363 250. 85 pp. MF–01; PC not available EDRS.

———. 1996. *Minorities in Higher Education: Fourteenth Annual Status Report*. Washington, D.C: American Council on Education. ED 407 892. 93 pp. MF–01; PC–04.

Chang, M.J. 1996. "Racial Diversity in Higher Education: Does a Racially Mixed Student Population Affect Educational Outcomes?" Ph.D. dissertation, Univ. of California at Los Angeles.

Chickering, A.W. 1969. *Education and Identity*. San Francisco: Jossey-Bass.

Chickering, A.W., and L. Reisser. 1993. *Education and Identity*. 2d ed. San Franciso: Jossey-Bass.

Collins, P.H. 1986. "Learning from the Outsider Within: The Sociological Significance of Black Feminist Thought." *Social Problems* 33(3): 514–32.

Cox, T., Jr. 1993. *Cultural Diversity in Organizations: Theory, Research, and Practice*. San Francisco: Berrett-Koehler.

Cross, W.E., Jr. 1971. "The Negro-to-Black Conversion Experience: Towards a Psychology of Black Liberation." *Black World* 20(9): 13–27.

———. 1978. "The Cross and Thomas Models of Psychological Nigrescence." *Journal of Black Psychology* 5(1): 13–31.

———. 1991. *Shades of Black: Diversity in African-American Identity*. Philadelphia: Temple Univ. Press.

Cross, W.E., Jr., T.A. Parham, and J.E. Helms. 1991. "The Stages of Black Identity Development: Nigrescence Models." In *Black Psychology*, edited by R. Jones. 3d ed. San Francisco: Cobb & Henry.

Crosson, P.H. 1988. "Four-Year College and University Environments for Minority Degree Achievement." *Review of Higher Education* 11(4): 365–82.

Davis, E.B. 1993. "Desegregation in Higher Education: Twenty-five Years of Controversy from *Geier* to *Ayers."Journal of Law and Education* 22(4): 519–24.

Davis, R. 1991. "Social Support Networks and Undergraduate Student Academic-Success-Related Outcomes: A Comparison of Black Students on Black and White Campuses." In *College in Black and White: African-American Students in Predominantly White and in Historically Black Public Universities,* edited by W.R. Allen, E.G. Epps, and N.Z. Haniff. Albany, N.Y.: SUNY Press.

Deppe, M. 1989. "The Impact of Racial Diversity and Involvement on College Students' Social Concern Values." Paper presented at an annual meeting of the Association for the Study of Higher

Education, Atlanta, Georgia.

Dey, E.L. 1996. "Undergraduate Political Attitudes: An Examination of Peer, Faculty, and Social Influences." *Research in Higher Education* 37(5): 535–54.

———. 1997. "Undergraduate Political Attitudes: Peer Influence in Changing Social Contexts." *Journal of Higher Education* 68(4): 398–413.

Dey, E.L., S. Rosevear, C. Navia, and R.D. Murphy. 1996. *The Miami University Campus Climate: Findings from Four Campus-wide Surveys.* Ann Arbor, Mich.: Center for the Study of Higher and Postsecondary Education.

Durán, R.P. 1983. *Hispanics' Education and Background: Predictors of College Achievement.* New York: College Board Publications.

Duster, T. 1993. "The Diversity of California at Berkeley: An Emerging Reformulation of 'Competence' in an Increasingly Multicultural World." In *Beyond a Dream Deferred: Multicultural Education and the Politics of Excellence,* edited by B.W. Thompson and S. Tyagi. Minneapolis: Univ. of Minnesota Press.

El-Khawas, E. 1989. *Campus Trends, 1989.* Higher Education Panel Reports No. 78. Washington, D.C.: American Council on Education. ED 310 700. 84 pp. MF–01; PC–04.

Farrell, W.C., Jr., and C.K. Jones. 1988. "Recent Racial Incidents in Higher Education: A Preliminary Perspective." *Urban Review* 20(3): 211–33.

Feldman, K.A., and T.M. Newcomb. 1969. *The Impact of College on Students.* Vol. 1. San Francisco: Jossey-Bass.

Gilliard, M.D. 1996. "Racial Climate and Institutional Support Factors Affecting Success in Predominantly White Institutions: An Examination of African-American and White Student Experiences." Ph.D. dissertation, Univ. of Michigan.

Globetti, E.C., G. Globetti, C.L. Brown, and R.E. Smith. 1993. "Social Interaction and Multiculturalism." *NASPA Journal* 30(3): 209–18.

Green, K.C. 1982. "The Impact of Neighborhood and Secondary School Integration on Educational Achievement and Occupational Attainment of College-Bound Blacks." Ph.D. dissertation, Univ. of California at Los Angeles.

Green, M.F., ed. 1989. *Minorities on Campus: A Handbook for Enhancing Diversity.* Washington, D.C.: American Council on Education.

Haniff, N.Z. 1991. "Epilogue." In *College in Black and White: African-American Students in Predominantly White and in Historically Black Public Universities.* edited by W.R. Allen, E.G.

Epps, and N.Z. Haniff. Albany, N.Y.: SUNY Press.

Helms, J. 1990. *Black and White Racial Identity: Theory, Research, and Practice*. Westport, Conn.: Greenwood Press.

Hsia, J. 1988. "Asian Americans Fight the Myth of the Super Student." *Educational Record* 68(4): 94–97.

Huffman, T.E. 1991. "The Experiences, Perceptions, and Consequences of Campus Racism among Northern Plains Indians." *Journal of American Indian Education* 30(2): 25–34.

Hurtado, S. 1990. "Campus Racial Climates and Educational Outcomes." Ph.D. dissertation, Univ. of California at Los Angeles.

————. 1992. "The Campus Racial Climate: Contexts for Conflict." *Journal of Higher Education* 63(5): 539–69.

————. 1993. "The Institutional Climate for Talented Latino Students." *Research in Higher Education* 35(1): 21–41.

————. 1997. "Linking Diversity and Educational Purpose: College Outcomes Associated with Diversity in the Faculty and Student Body." Paper presented at a conference of the Harvard Civil Rights Project, Cambridge, Massachusetts.

Hurtado, S., D.F. Carter, and S. Sharp. 1995. "Social Interaction on Campus: Differences among Self-Perceived Ability Groups." Paper presented at a meeting of the Association for Institutional Research, Boston, Massachusetts. ED 387 014. 38 pp. MF–01; PC–02.

Hurtado, S., D.F. Carter, and A. Spuler. 1996. "Latino Student Transition to College." *Research in Higher Education* 37(2): 135–57.

Hurtado, S., E. Dey, and J. Treviño. 1994. "Exclusion or Self-Segregation? Interaction across Racial/Ethnic Groups on College Campuses." Paper presented at a conference of the American Educational Research Association, New Orleans, Louisiana.

Hurtado, S., J.F. Milem, A. Clayton-Pedersen, and W.A. Allen. 1998. "Enhancing Campus Climates for Racial/Ethnic Diversity: Educational Policy and Practice." *Review of Higher Education* 21(3): 279–302.

Institute for the Study of Social Change. 1991. "Diversity Project." Berkeley, Calif.: Author.

Jackman, M.R. 1978. "General and Applied Tolerance: Does Education Increase Commitment to Racial Integration?" *American Journal of Political Science* 22: 302–24.

Jackman, M.R., and M.J. Muha. 1984. "Education and Intergroup Attitudes: Moral Enlightenment, Superficial Democratic Commitment, or Ideological Refinement?" *American Sociological Review* 49: 751–69.

Jackson, K.W., and L.A. Swan. 1991. "Institutional and Individual

Factors Affecting Black Undergraduate Student Performance: Campus Race and Student Gender." In *College in Black and White: African-American Students in Predominantly White and in Historically Black Public Universities,* edited by W.R. Allen, E.G. Epps, and N.Z. Haniff. Albany, N.Y.: SUNY Press.

Kanter, R.M. 1977. "Some Effects of Proportions on Group Life: Skewed Sex Ratios and Responses to Token Women." *American Journal of Sociology* 82: 965–89.

Kluegel, J.R., and L. Bobo. August 1993. "Opposition to Race-Targeting: Self-Interest, Stratification Ideology, or Racial Attitudes?" *American Sociological Review* 58(4): 443–64.

Kuh, G., J.S. Schuh, E.J. Whitt, R.E. Andreas, J.W. Lyons, C.C. Strange, L.E. Krehbiel, and K.A. MacKay. 1991. *Involving Colleges: Successful Approaches to Fostering Student Learning and Personal Development outside the Classroom.* San Francisco: Jossey-Bass.

Lawrence, J., and R. Blackburn. 1985. "Faculty Careers: Maturation, Demographic, and Historical Effects." *Research in Higher Education* 22(2): 135–54.

Levine, A., and J. Cureton. 1992. "The Quiet Revolution: Eleven Facts about Multiculturalism and the Curriculum." *Change* 24(1): 25–29.

Lin, R.L., D. LaCounte, and J. Elder. 1988. "A Study of Native American Students in a Predominantly White College." *Journal of American Indian Education* 27(3): 8–15.

Loo, C.M., and G. Rolison. 1986. "Alienation of Ethnic Minority Students at a Predominately White University." *Journal of Higher Education* 57: 58–77.

McGregor, J. 1993. "Effectiveness of Role Playing and Antiracist Teaching in Reducing Student Prejudice." *Journal of Educational Research* 86(4): 215–26.

MacPhee, D., J.C. Kreutzer, and J.J. Fritz. 1994. "Infusing a Diversity Perspective into Human Development Courses." *Child Development* 65(2): 699–715.

Marcus, L.R., and D.K. Yavorsky. September 1989. "Improving Human Relations on Campus: The Role of State-Level Policy." In *Minority Success: A Policy Report of the State Higher Education Executive Officers Minority Student Achievement Project.* Denver: SHEEO.

Matthews, D. 1996. "Changing State and Federal Roles in Improving Minority Education." In *Educating a New Majority: Transforming America's Educational System for Diversity,* edited by L.I. Rendon, R.O. Hope, and Associates. San Francisco: Jossey-Bass.

Milem, J.F. 1992. "The Impact of College on Students' Racial Attitudes and Levels of Racial Awareness." Doctoral dissertation, Univ. of California at Los Angeles.

———. 1994a. "Attitude Change in College Students: Examining the Effect of College Peer Groups and Faculty Normative Groups." Paper presented at an annual meeting of the Association for the Study of Higher Education, Tucson, Arizona.

———. 1994b. "College, Students, and Racial Understanding." *Thought and Action* (9)2: 51–92.

Milem, J.F., and H.S. Astin. 1993. "The Changing Composition of Faculty: What Does It Really Mean for Diversity?" *Change* 25(2): 21–27.

Minatoya, L.Y., and W.E. Sedlacek. 1980. "Background and Attitude. Toward Interracial Contact: A Profile of Black and White University Students." *Integrated Education* 19(5–6): 43–45.

Mitchell, S.L., and D.M. Dell. 1992. "The Relationship between Black Students' Racial Identity Attitude and Participation in Campus Organizations." *Journal of College Student Development* 33: 39–43.

Muñoz, C. 1989. *Youth, Identity, and Power in the Chicano Movement.* New York: Verso.

Myrdal, G. 1944. *An American Dilemma.* New York: Harper.

National Task Force for Minority Achievement in Higher Education. 1990. "Achieving Campus Diversity: Policies for Change." Denver: Education Commission of the States. ED 329 178. 50 pp. MF–01; PC–02.

Nettles, M.T. 1991. "Racial Similarities and Differences in the Predictors of College Student Achievement." In *College in Black and White: African-American Students in Predominantly White and in Historically Black Public Universities,* edited by W.R. Allen, E.G. Epps, and N.Z. Haniff. Albany, N.Y.: SUNY Press.

———, ed. 1988. *Toward Black Undergraduate Student Equality in American Higher Education.* Westport, Conn.: Greenwood Press.

Newcomb, T.M. 1966. "The General Nature of Peer Group Influence." In *College Peer Groups,* edited by T.M. Newcomb and E.K. Wilson. Chicago: Aldine–National Opinion Research Center.

Newcomb, T.M., and E.K. Wilson, eds. 1966. *College Peer Groups.* Chicago: Aldine–National Opinion Research Center.

Nora, A., and A.F. Cabrera. 1996. "The Role of Perceptions of Prejudice and Discrimination on the Adjustment of Minority Students to College." *Journal of Higher Education* 67(2): 119–48.

O'Brien, E.M. 1992. "American Indians in Higher Education." *Research Briefs* 3(3). Washington, D.C.: American Council on

Education.

Olivas, M.A. 1986. "The Retreat from Access." *Academe* 72: 16–18.

Orfield, G. 1992. "Money, Equity, and College Access." *Harvard Educational Review* 62(3): 337–72.

Ortiz, A.M. 1995. "Promoting Racial Understanding in College Students: A Study of Educational and Developmental Interventions." Paper presented at an annual meeting of the Association for the Study of Higher Education, Orlando, Florida.

Palmer, P.J. 1987. "Community, Conflict, and Ways of Knowing." *Change* 19(5): 20–25.

Parham, T.A. 1989. "Cycles of Psychological Nigrescence." *The Counseling Psychologist* 17(2): 187–226.

Pascarella, E.T., M. Edison, A. Nora, L.S. Hagedorn, and P.T. Terenzini. 1996. "Influences on Students' Openness to Diversity and Challenge in the First Year of College." *Journal of Higher Education* 67(2): 174–95.

Pascarella, E.T., and P.T. Terenzini. 1991. *How College Affects Students: Findings and Insights from Twenty Years of Research*. San Francisco: Jossey-Bass.

Pascarella, E.T., E.J. Whitt, A. Nora, M. Edison, L.S. Hagedorn, and P.T. Terenzini. 1996. "What Have We Learned from the First Year of the National Study of Student Learning?" *Journal of College Student Development* 37(2): 182–92.

Peterson, M.W., R.T. Blackburn, Z.F. Gamson, C.H. Arce, R.W. Davenport, and J.R. Mingle. 1978. *Black Students on White Campuses: The Impacts of Increased Black Enrollments*. Ann Arbor, Mich.: Institute for Social Research.

Peterson, M.W., and M.G. Spencer. 1990. "Understanding Academic Culture and Climate." In *Assessing Academic Climates and Cultures,* edited by W.G. Tierney. New Directions for Institutional Research No. 68. San Francisco: Jossey-Bass.

Prillerman, S.L., H.F. Myers, and B.D. Smedley. 1989. "Stress, Well-Being, and Academic Achievement in College." In *Black Students: Psychosocial Issues and Academic Achievement,* edited by G.L. Berry and J.K. Asamen. Newbury Park, Calif.: Sage.

Richardson, R., D. Matthews, and B. Finney. 1992. *Improving State and Campus Environments for Quality and Diversity: A Self-Assessment*. Denver: Education Commission of the States.

Richardson, R., and E. Skinner. 1991. *Achieving Diversity*. Washington, D.C.: ACE/Macmillan.

St. John, E.P. 1990. "Price Response in Enrollment Decisions: An Analysis of the High School and Beyond Sophomore Cohort." *Research in Higher Education* 31(2): 161–76.

————. 1991a. "The Impact of Student Financial Aid: A Review of Recent Research." *Journal of Student Financial Aid* 21(1): 18–32.

————. 1991b. "What Really Influences Minority Attendance? Sequential Analyses of the High School and Beyond Sophomore Cohort." *Research in Higher Education* 32(2): 141–58.

St. John, E.P., and C.L. Masten. 1990. "Return on Investment in Student Financial Aid: An Assessment for the High School Class of 1972." *Journal of Student Financial Aid* 20(3): 4–23.

Sampson, William A. 1986. "Desegregation and Racial Tolerance in Academia." *Journal of Negro Education* 55(2): 171–84.

Sandler, B. 1987. "The Classroom Climate: Still a Chilly One for Women." In *Educating Men and Women Together,* edited by C. Lasser. Carbondale: Univ. of Illinois.

Sandler, B., and R.M. Hall. 1982. "The Classroom Climate: A Chilly One for Women?" Washington, D.C.: Association of American Colleges. ED 215 628. 24 pp. MF–01; PC–01.

Schoem, D. 1997. "Intergroup Relations, Conflict, and Community." In *Democratic Education in an Age of Difference: Redesigning Citizenship in Higher Education,* edited by R. Guarasci, G.H. Cornwell, and Associates. San Francisco: Jossey-Bass.

Schuman, H., C. Steeh, and L. Bobo. 1985. *Racial Attitudes in America.* Cambridge, Mass.: Harvard Univ. Press.

Scott, E.S., and S.B. Damico. 1982. "Predictors of Interracial Contact for High School and University Students." ED 216 091. 15 pp. MF–01; PC–01.

Scott, R.R., and J.M. McPartland. 1982. "Desegregation as National Policy: Correlates of Racial Attitudes." *American Educational Research Journal* 19(3): 397–414.

Sedlacek, W. 1987. "Black Students on White Campuses: 20 Years of Research." *Journal of College Student Personnel* 28(6): 484–95.

Sedlacek, W.E., and G.C. Brooks, Jr. 1976. *Racism in American Education.* Chicago: Nelson-Hall.

Singer, E. 1981. "Reference Groups and Social Evaluations." In *Social Psychology: Sociological Perspectives,* edited by M. Rosenberg and R.H. Turner. New York: Basic Books.

Slavin, R.E. 1985. "Cooperative Learning: Applying Contact Theory in Desegregated Schools." *Journal of Social Issues* 41(1): 45–62.

Smedley, B.D., H.F. Myers, and S.P. Harrell. 1993. "Minority-Status Stresses and the College Adjustment of Ethnic Minority Freshmen." *Journal of Higher Education* 64(4): 434–52.

Smith, D.G. 1989. *The Challenge of Diversity: Involvement or Alienation in the Academy?* ASHE-ERIC Higher Education Report No. 5. Washington, D.C.: George Washington Univ., Graduate School of Education and Human Development. ED 314 987. 129 pp. MF–01; PC–06.

Smith, D.G., and Associates. 1997. *Diversity Works: The Emerging Picture of How Students Benefit.* Washington, D.C.: Association of American Colleges and Universities. ED 416 797. 159 pp. MF–01; PC not available EDRS.

Southern Education Foundation. 1995. *Redeeming the American Promise: Report of the Panel on Educational Opportunity and Postsecondary Desegregation.* Atlanta: Author. ED 383 225. 157 pp. MF–01; PC–07.

Springer, L., B. Palmer, P.T. Terenzini, E.T. Pascarella, and A. Nora. 1996. "Attitudes toward Campus Diversity: Participation in a Racial or Cultural Awareness Workshop." *Review of Higher Education* 20(1): 53–68.

Stampen, J.O. 1985. *Student Aid and Public Higher Education: Recent Changes.* Washington, D.C.: American Association of State Colleges and Universities. ED 353 900. 125 pp. MF–01; PC–05.

Stampen, J.O., and R.H. Fenske. 1988. "The Impact of Financial Aid on Ethnic Minorities." *Review of Higher Education* 11(4): 337–53.

State Higher Education Executive Officers, Task Force on Minority Achievement. 1987. *A Difference of Degrees: State Inititiatives to Improve Higher Education.* Denver: Author. ED 287 355. 75 pp. MF–01; PC–03.

Steele, C.M. April 1992. "Race and the Schooling of Black Americans." *Atlantic Monthly:* 68–78.

Stephan, W.G., and C.W. Stephan. 1985. "Intergroup Anxiety." *Journal of Social Issues* 41(3): 157–75.

Stewart, J.B. 1991. "Planning for Cultural Diversity: A Case Study." In *Cultural Pluralism on Campus,* edited by Harold E. Cheatham. Washington, D.C.: American College Personnel Association.

Suzuki, B.H. 1994. "Higher Education Issues in the Asian American Community." In *Minorities in Higher Education,* edited by M.J. Justiz, R. Wilson, and L.G. Björk. Phoenix: Oryx.

Takagi, D.Y. 1992. *The Retreat from Race: Asian American Admissions and Racial Politics.* New Brunswick, N.J.: Rutgers Univ. Press.

Tatum, D. 1992. "Talking about Race, Learning about Racism: The Application of Racial Identity Development Theory in the Classroom." *Harvard Educational Review* 62(1): 1–24.

Terenzini, P., L. Rendón, L. Upcraft, S. Millar, K. Allison, P. Gregg, and J. Jalomo. 1994. "The Transition to College: Diverse Students, Diverse Stories." *Research in Higher Education* 35(1): 57–73.

Thelin, J. 1985. "Beyond the Background Music: Historical Research on Admissions and Access in Higher Education." In *Higher Education Handbook of Theory and Research,* edited by J.C. Smart. Vol. 1. New York: Agathon.

Thomas, G.E., and F. Brown. 1982. "What Does Educational Research Tell Us about School Desegregation Effects?" *Journal of Black Studies* 13(2): 155–74.

Thomas, G.E., and J. McPartland. 1984. "Have College Desegregation Policies Threatened Black Student Enrollment and Black Colleges? An Empirical Analysis." *Journal of Negro Education* 53(4): 389–99.

Tierney, W.G. 1987. "Facts and Constructs: Defining Reality in Higher Education Organizations." *Review of Higher Education* 11(1): 61–73.

Tinto, V. 1987. *Leaving College: Rethinking the Causes and Cures of Student Attrition.* Chicago: Univ. of Chicago Press.

———. 1993. *Leaving College: Rethinking the Causes and Cures of Student Attrition.* 2d ed. Chicago: Univ. of Chicago Press.

Tracey, T.J., and W.E. Sedlacek. 1985. "The Relationship of Non-cognitive Variables to Cognitive Success: A Longitudinal Comparison by Race." *Journal of College Student Personnel* 26: 405–10.

Treisman, P.U. 1992. "Studying Students Studying Calculus: A Look at the Lives of Minority Mathematics Students in College." *College Mathematics Journal* 23(5): 362–72.

Treviño, J.G. 1992. "Participating in Ethnic/Racial Student Organizations." Ph.D. dissertation, Univ. of California at Los Angeles.

Trujillo, C.J. 1986. "A Comparative Examination of Classroom Interactons between Professors and Minority and Nonminority College Students." *American Educational Research Journal* 23(4): 629–42.

Turner, C. 1994. "Guests in Someone Else's House: Students of Color." *Review of Higher Education* 17(4): 355–70.

———. 1997. "Welcoming Diversity on Campus: The Need for Transformation of University Culture." Working paper of the Interdisciplinary Program in Public Policy and Minority Communities. Minneapolis: Univ. of Minnnesota.

Washington State Higher Education Coordinating Board. 1991. "Policy on Minority Participation and Diversity." Olympia: Author.

Weidman, J.C. 1989. "Undergraduate Socialization: A Conceptual Approach." In *Handbook of Research in Higher Education,* edited by J.C. Smart. Vol. 5. New York: Agathon.

Weiner, S. 1992. "Are Friendships Enough? Student Race Relations on Four Campuses." *AAHE Bulletin* 45(4): 8–11.

Whitt, E.J., M.I. Edison, E.T. Pascarella, P.T. Terenzini, and A. Nora. 1998. "Influences on Students' Openness to Diversity and Challenge in the Second and Third Year of College." Paper presented at an annual meeting of the Association for the Study of Higher Education, Miami, Florida.

Williams, John B., III. 1988. "Title VI Regulation of Higher Education." In *Desegregating America's Colleges and Universities,* edited by J.B. Williams III. New York: Teachers College Press.

Zisman, P., and V. Wilson. 1992. "Table Hopping in the Cafeteria: An Exploration of 'Racial' Integration in Early Adolescent Social Groups." *Anthropology and Education Quarterly* 23: 199–220.

Zúñiga, X., and B.A. Nagda. 1992. "Dialogue Groups: An Innovative Approach to Multicultural Learning." In *Multicultural Teaching at the University,* edited by David Schoem. New York: Praeger.

INDEX

A

attitude, development of in college, 28–36

    peers, influence of, 28–31

    racial, role of education, contacts, and campus activities, 32–36

    reference groups, 28–31

B

behavioral dimension, 4, 6, 37–54

C

campus activities, effects on racial attitude, 32–36

campus support systems, 54

classroom diversity, approaches to, 45–49

classroom environment, link with social interaction, 40–44

Conflict Mediation Program, 84–86

contacts, effects on racial attitude, 32–36

curricular change, approaches to, 45–49

D

desegregation, 9–14

    and institutional mission, 9–14

    legislation and litigation, 10–14

    research on the effects of, 14–17

Design for Diversity, 91–93

design principals for greater diversity, 69–77

    key components, 73

    12 research-based, 70–77, 93–95

discrimination, the impact on students, 25–28

diverse peer groups, contact with, and educational outcomes, 52–54

Diversity Discussion Workbook, 90–91

diversity emphasis, 56–57

diversity, in higher education institutions, 69–78

    behavioral, 37–54

    psychological, 25–36

    social, 49–52

    structural, 19–24

Diversity Opportunity Tool, 88–89

E

education, its role in racial attitude, 32–36

exclusion, in learning environments, 9

historical legacy of, 9

F

faculty, diversifying on campus, 22–24
    as a reference group, 28–32
financial aid, effects on diversity in students, 63–67

H

historical legacy, 4, 5, 9–17

I

inclusion, in learning environments, 9
    historical legacy of, 9
institutional climate, 3–7, 37–54, 55–67
    conceptualizing, 3–7
    effect on social interaction, 49–52
    learning environment, 55–67
institutional mission, desegregation, 9
intergroup dialogues, 86–88
Intergroup Relations Center, 81–83
Intergroup Relations, Conflict, and Community, 86–88

L

learning environment, general, 55–67
    link with institutional climate, 55–67
    link with learning environment, 55–67
legislation and litigation on desegregation, 10–14

M

minority support programs, participation in, 54
multimedia packages on dispute resolution and diversity, 83–84

P

peer groups, diverse, 36, 52–54
practice of diversity on campuses, 79–96
    examples of, 79–93
    Arizona State University, 81–83
    Carnegie Mellon University, 83–84
    Ohio State University, 90–91
    University of California at Los Angeles, 84–86
    University of Michigan, 86–88
    University of North Carolina, 90–91
    University of Washington, 90–91

University of Wisconsin system, 91–93
Vanderbilt University, 88–89
prejudice, reduction of in college, 28–36
psychological climate, 4, 5, 25–36
    research on, 27–28

R

race relations on campus, 49–52
racial demography, 15–17
racial/ethnic student organizations, participation in, 54

S

social interaction, link with classroom environment, 40–44
social interaction on campus, 49–52
    effect on race relations, 49–52
state policy makers, role of, 57–63
state policy, role in improving climate, 57–63
structural diversity, 4, 5
    impact of, 19–24
student enrollments and increased complexity, 19–22
student involvement, effects of behavioral dimension, 37–40

W

Washington Higher Education Coordinating Board, 61

ASHE-ERIC HIGHER EDUCATION REPORTS

Since 1983, the Association for the Study of Higher Education (ASHE) and the Educational Resources Information Center (ERIC) Clearinghouse on Higher Education, a sponsored project of the Graduate School of Education and Human Development at The George Washington University, have cosponsored the ASHE-ERIC Higher Education Report series. This volume is the twenty-sixth overall and the ninth to be published by the Graduate School of Education and Human Development at The George Washington University.

Each monograph is the definitive analysis of a tough higher education problem, based on thorough research of pertinent literature and institutional experiences. Topics are identified by a national survey. Noted practitioners and scholars are then commissioned to write the reports, with experts providing critical reviews of each manuscript before publication.

Eight monographs (10 before 1985) in the ASHE-ERIC Higher Education Report series are published each year and are available on individual and subscription bases. To order, use the order form on the last page of this book.

Qualified persons interested in writing a monograph for the ASHE-ERIC Higher Education Report series are invited to submit a proposal to the National Advisory Board. As the preeminent literature review and issue analysis series in higher education, the Higher Education Reports are guaranteed wide dissemination and national exposure for accepted candidates. Execution of a monograph requires at least a minimal familiarity with the ERIC database, including *Resources in Education* and the current *Index to Journals in Education*. The objective of these reports is to bridge conventional wisdom with practical research. Prospective authors are strongly encouraged to call at (800) 773-3742 ext. 14.

For further information, write to
    ASHE-ERIC Higher Education Report Series
    The George Washington University
    One Dupont Circle, Suite 630
    Washington, DC 20036-1183
Or phone (202) 296-2597
Toll free: (800) 773-ERIC

    Write or call for a complete catalog.

    Visit our Web site at **www.eriche.org/reports**

Barbara Lee
Rutgers University

Ivan B. Liss
Radford University

Anne Goodsell Love
University of Akron

Clara M. Lovett
Northern Arizona University

Meredith Ludwig
Education Statistics Services Institute

Jean MacGregor
Evergreen State College

William McKeachie
University of Michigan

Laurence R. Marcus
Rowan College

Mantha V. Mehallis
Florida Atlantic University

Robert Menges
Northwestern University

John A. Muffo
Virginia Polytechnic Institute and State University

Patricia H. Murrell
University of Memphis

L. Jackson Newell
Deep Springs College

Steven G. Olswang
University of Washington

Sherry Sayles-Folks
Eastern Michigan University

Maria Scatena
St. Mary of the Woods College

John Schuh
Iowa State University

Carole Schwinn
Jackson Community College

Patricia Somers
University of Arkansas at Little Rock

Leonard Springer
University of Wisconsin–Madison

Edward P. St. John
The University of Dayton

Marilla D. Svinicki
University of Texas–Austin

David Sweet
OERI, U.S. Department of Education

Jon E. Travis
Texas A&M University

Caroline Sotello Viernes Turner
University of Minnesota

Christine K. Wilkinson
Arizona State University

Donald H. Wulff
University of Washington

Manta Yorke
Liverpool John Moores University

William Zeller
University of Michigan at Ann Arbor

REVIEW PANEL

Richard Alfred
University of Michigan

Robert J. Barak
Iowa State Board of Regents

Alan Bayer
Virginia Polytechnic Institute and State University

John P. Bean
Indiana University–Bloomington

John M. Braxton
Peabody College, Vanderbilt University

Ellen M. Brier
Tennessee State University

Dennis Brown
University of Kansas

Patricia Carter
University of Michigan

John A. Centra
Syracuse University

Paul B. Chewning
Council for the Advancement and Support of Education

Arthur W. Chickering
Vermont College

Darrel A. Clowes
Virginia Polytechnic Institute and State University

Deborah M. DiCroce
Piedmont Virginia Community College

Dorothy E. Finnegan
The College of William & Mary

Kenneth C. Green
Claremont Graduate University

James C. Hearn
University of Georgia

Edward R. Hines
Illinois State University

Deborah Hunter
University of Vermont

Linda K. Johnsrud
University of Hawaii at Manoa

Bruce Anthony Jones
University of Missouri–Columbia

Elizabeth A. Jones
West Virginia University

Marsha V. Krotseng
State College and University Systems of West Virginia

George D. Kuh
Indiana University–Bloomington

J. Roderick Lauver
Planned Systems International, Inc.–Maryland

Daniel T. Layzell
MGT of America, Inc., Madison, Wisconsin

Patrick G. Love
Kent State University

Meredith Jane Ludwig
American Association of State Colleges and Universities

Mantha V. Mehallis
Florida Atlantic University

Toby Milton
Essex Community College

John A. Muffo
Virginia Polytechnic Institute and State University

L. Jackson Newell
Deep Springs College

Mark Oromaner
Hudson Community College

James C. Palmer
Illinois State University

Robert A. Rhoads
Michigan State University

G. Jeremiah Ryan
Quincy College

Mary Ann Danowitz Sagaria
The Ohio State University

Kathryn Nemeth Tuttle
University of Kansas

Volume 26 ASHE-ERIC Higher Education Reports

1. Faculty Workload Studies: Perspectives, Needs, and Future
   Directions
   Katrina A. Meyer

2. Assessing Faculty Publication Productivity: Issues of Equity
   Elizabeth G. Creamer

3. Proclaiming and Sustaining Excellence: Assessment as a
   Faculty Role
   Karen Maitland Schilling and Karl L. Schilling

4. Creating Learning Centered Classrooms: What Does Learning
   Theory Have to Say?
   *Frances K. Stage, Patricia A. Muller, Jillian Kinzie, and
   Ada Simmons*

5. The Academic Administrator and the Law: What Every Dean
   and Department Chair Needs to Know
   J. Douglas Toma and Richard L. Palm

6. The Powerful Potential of Learning Communities:
   Improving Education for the Future
   Oscar T. Lenning and Larry H. Ebbers

7. Enrollment Management for the 21st Century: Institutional
   Goals, Accountability, and Fiscal Responsibility
   Garlene Penn

Volume 25 ASHE-ERIC Higher Education Reports

1. A Culture for Academic Excellence: Implementing the Quality
   Principles in Higher Education
   Jann E. Freed, Marie R. Klugman, and Jonathan D. Fife

2. From Discipline to Development: Rethinking Student Conduct in Higher Education
   Michael Dannells

3. Academic Controversy: Enriching College Instruction through
   Intellectual Conflict
   David W. Johnson, Roger T. Johnson, and Karl A. Smith

4. Higher Education Leadership: Analyzing the Gender Gap
   Luba Chliwniak

5. The Virtual Campus: Technology and Reform in Higher
   Education
   Gerald C. Van Dusen

6. Early Intervention Programs: Opening the Door to Higher
   Education
   *Robert H. Fenske, Christine A. Geranios, Jonathan E.
   Keller, and David E. Moore*

7. The Vitality of Senior Faculty Members: Snow on the Roof—
   Fire in the Furnace
   Carole J. Bland and William H. Bergquist

---

8. A National Review of Scholastic Achievement in General Education: How Are We Doing and Why Should We Care?
Steven J. Osterlind

Volume 24 ASHE-ERIC Higher Education Reports

1. Tenure, Promotion, and Reappointment: Legal and Administrative Implications
Benjamin Baez and John A. Centra

2. Taking Teaching Seriously: Meeting the Challenge of Instructional Improvement
Michael B. Paulsen and Kenneth A. Feldman

3. Empowering the Faculty: Mentoring Redirected and Renewed
Gaye Luna and Deborah L. Cullen

4. Enhancing Student Learning: Intellectual, Social, and Emotional Integration
Anne Goodsell Love and Patrick G. Love

5. Benchmarking in Higher Education: Adapting Best Practices to Improve Quality
Jeffrey W. Alstete

6. Models for Improving College Teaching: A Faculty Resource
Jon E. Travis

7. Experiential Learning in Higher Education: Linking Classroom and Community
Jeffrey A. Cantor

8. Successful Faculty Development and Evaluation: The Complete Teaching Portfolio
John P. Murray

Volume 23 ASHE-ERIC Higher Education Reports

1. The Advisory Committee Advantage: Creating an Effective Strategy for Programmatic Improvement
Lee Teitel

2. Collaborative Peer Review: The Role of Faculty in Improving College Teaching
Larry Keig and Michael D. Waggoner

3. Prices, Productivity, and Investment: Assessing Financial Strategies in Higher Education
Edward P. St. John

4. The Development Officer in Higher Education: Toward an Understanding of the Role
Michael J. Worth and James W. Asp II

5. Measuring Up: The Promises and Pitfalls of Performance Indicators in Higher Education
Gerald Gaither, Brian P. Nedwek, and John E. Neal

6. A New Alliance: Continuous Quality and Classroom
   Effectiveness
   Mimi Wolverton

7. Redesigning Higher Education: Producing Dramatic Gains in
   Student Learning
   Lion F. Gardiner

8. Student Learning outside the Classroom: Transcending
   Artificial Boundaries
   *George D. Kuh, Katie Branch Douglas, Jon P. Lund, and
   Jackie Ramin-Gyurnek*

Volume 22 ASHE-ERIC Higher Education Reports

1. The Department Chair: New Roles, Responsibilities, and
   Challenges
   Alan T. Seagren, John W. Creswell, and Daniel W. Wheeler

2. Sexual Harassment in Higher Education: From Conflict to
   Community
   *Robert O. Riggs, Patricia H. Murrell, and JoAnne C.
   Cutting*

3. Chicanos in Higher Education: Issues and Dilemmas for the
   21st Century
   Adalberto Aguirre, Jr., and Ruben O. Martinez

4. Academic Freedom in American Higher Education: Rights,
   Responsibilities, and Limitations
   Robert K. Poch

5. Making Sense of the Dollars: The Costs and Uses of Faculty
   Compensation
   Kathryn M. Moore and Marilyn J. Amey

6. Enhancing Promotion, Tenure, and Beyond: Faculty
   Socialization as a Cultural Process
   William G. Tierney and Robert A. Rhoads

7. New Perspectives for Student Affairs Professionals: Evolving
   Realities, Responsibilities, and Roles
   Peter H. Garland and Thomas W. Grace

8. Turning Teaching into Learning: The Role of Student
   Responsibility in the Collegiate Experience
   Todd M. Davis and Patricia Hillman Murrell